D0067131

THE WISDOM OF
WALK-ONS

7 WINNING STRATEGIES FOR
COLLEGE, BUSINESS AND LIFE

Paul L. Corona, MBA, EdD

ISBN-10: 1439286442
EAN-13: 9781439286449

Library of Congress Control Number: 2012904395
CreateSpace, North Charleston, SC

PRAISE FOR THE WISDOM OF WALK-ONS

"If you want more out of your personal and professional lives, then *The WoW* is a must-read. Original, penetrating and alive with tremendous insight, this instant classic captures the true stories and winning strategies of three underdogs who beat the odds at every turn. It's one of the best sports books I've ever read."

—James O'Connor

Retired Group Vice President of Marketing, Sales and Service
Ford Motor Company

"*The WoW* blends the unique excitement of major college football with three true stories of underdogs whose passion to succeed against overwhelming odds is truly inspirational. Corona combines these special stories with his seven winning strategies for success and encourages us all to push the limits of our potential in our careers and personal lives."

—Kelly Ryan

Quarterback, Captain and Ivy League MVP Yale University, 1987
Partner – Quiet Light Trading LLC

"Every life has its challenges. Every person has dreams or goals that they feel are just beyond reach. Every worthwhile pursuit requires perseverance, adaptability and resilience to be achieved. Using life histories of walk-on college athletes as a foundation, Paul Corona derives simple strategies for leading a successful life. Pithy, practical and truly engaging, *The Wisdom of Walk-Ons* presents strategies we all can use. Tenacity, resilience, flexibility and a concern for others are virtues that serve us well in school, in sports and throughout life. Through his seven lessons of walk-ons, Corona shows us how these virtues can be developed. *The WoW* is a powerful book. Whenever one feels over-matched by a problem, this is a guide worth revisiting. After all, we're all walk-ons at one point or another."

—Mark Reinecke, PhD

Professor of Psychiatry & Behavioral Sciences and Chief Psychologist
Northwestern University's Feinberg School of Medicine

"*The WoW* does a great job of quenching our thirst for the underdog! Corona helps us relate to the character and commitment of three special athletes who pursued stretch goals on and off the field. This must-read ignites the fighting spirit inherent in us all."

—Tracey Maltby

Former personal assistant to Billie Jean King
Former Director of Media – World TeamTennis

"Experience three true stories of those who were told they wouldn't make it (but did anyway). Learn that it's not rocket science but an understanding of seven valuable lessons. Create your future with a practical action plan."

—Rich Teerlink

Retired Chairman and CEO
Harley-Davidson, Inc.

"*The Wisdom of Walk-Ons* delivers an engaging ride with three exceptional examples of what can be accomplished when you put your mind to it. Then it shows you how to apply the same strategies for your own success. Dr. Corona's story-telling is insightful, inspiring and compelling. Maybe most important, the lessons are broadly applicable."

—Ron Boe

Director of Multi-Media Sales
The Wall Street Journal

"I have read countless self-improvement books over the years and have never come across one like this. Paul Corona, in *The Wisdom of Walk-ons*, will make a true connection with anyone who is a sports fan or just has a desire to be more successful in all facets of life. He combines seven highly valuable success strategies with the backdrop of three inspiring underdog stories. If you are anything like me, once you start reading you won't be able stop! Stay tuned, one day Corona could be mentioned in the same breath as Carnegie, Blanchard and Covey."

—Steven Prue

Chairman and CEO
Prototech Laser, Inc.

"*The Wisdom of Walk-Ons* is an inspiring book about never giving up. Paul Corona does a masterful job of using three unheralded college football prospects to illustrate how anything is possible in life. These walk-ons used hard work and dedication to achieve their goals in college—and as a springboard to success later in life." (Coach Fracassa has over 400 career victories, which is the most of any coach in Michigan and number 10 nationally.)

—Albert Fracassa

Head Football Coach – Brother Rice High School
Bloomfield Hills, Michigan

"If you've spent any time at all in business, you've encountered the 'wisdom of walk-ons' Corona so deftly deciphers. They're the folks with the tenacity, the drive, the creativity and the resilience to lead when others waver. And quite often, you'll find them in the board room or the corner office. Paul's engaging story-telling connects the legendary lessons of college football's most iconic coaches to underdog ideas we can apply every day in business and management. Read it. You'll relate."

—Patrick Corry

Managing Director and Head of Brand Marketing
UBS Wealth Management

"Paul Corona's strengths as an inspirational coach shine through in this primer on self-improvement and personal achievement. Corona attacks the ethereal and thorny topic of motivation through the eyes of dreamers who dared to achieve, and he presents us with a front-row seat to observe some of the greatest coaching leaders of our time. Whether you want to achieve in business, school, sports or life in general, lessons abound in this easy-to-read book. Get it, and then get going."

—Sean Malinowski, PhD

Captain
Los Angeles Police Department

"If you want a clear map for success and love rooting for underdogs who win, you won't be able to put down this book. We employ many of *The WoW's* winning strategies at our corporate university."

—Mike Gerard

Chief Learning Officer
CBRE Group

"You'll marvel, as I did, at the inspiring stories of these three men and see that their life lessons are more about the world we all live in than about the world of football. *The WoW* breaks it down for you: how to combine your dream with practical steps to achieve it. Paul Corona knows people and how to help them reach."

—Perry Metz

General Manager
Indiana University's WTIU (PBS) and WFIU (NPR)

"Paul Corona is a champion for the underdog. *The Wisdom of Walk-Ons* gives an inspirational account of how hard work, commitment and dedication lead to success on the athletic field and in life. Dr. Corona's seven winning strategies serve as a great game plan for personal and professional achievement. Make sure you put this powerful book to good use!"

—Greg Wendt

Draftee – Boston Celtics, 1986
All Star Guard/Forward – German Professional League, 1991-94
Senior Account Manager – Premier Polymers, Inc.

"Profound in its simplicity, *The Wisdom of Walk-Ons* helps readers become more competitive and effective in business and life. Using the lessons of real people who have excelled against the odds, Corona challenges readers to raise their own game. Both instructional and inspirational, *The WoW* is a collection of valuable messages wrapped in great sports stories."

—Brenda Knapp, ACC

Executive Coach and Program Manager
WOMEN Unlimited,Inc.

"What can a college football walk-on teach us about life? Apparently everything. *The Wisdom of Walk-Ons* takes these unlikely teachers and deftly translates their gridiron successes into lives filled with success. These stimulating, vivid stories move as fast as the game of football and teach the seven strategies Corona has identified to help us achieve a balanced approach to family and career."

—Richard Salyer

Senior Vice President and Group Account Director
Cramer-Kraselt

"Corona's book stands apart from the field full of overly generic and academic self-help manuals on the market today. The stories of these former walk-ons combine an insider's look into the fascinating world of college football with a unique insight into their 'post glory days' business success. It's a compelling and truly helpful read that any businessperson can relate to. *The Wisdom of Walk-Ons* is a self-help book, maybe the only one, I will recommend on a regular basis."

—Tom Eiselt

Partner
A Big Four accounting and consulting firm

"Finally, a book that captures the necessary tools for success and puts them in a format that's entertaining and inspiring! Corona uses the backdrop of one of our nation's most cherished pastimes, college football, to hold our attention from cover to cover – and by doing so makes us better in our careers and, more importantly, in life."

—Michael Baxter

Vice President of Sales and Marketing
Freudenberg-NOK Group

"Masterfully crafted, *The Wisdom of Walk-Ons* extrapolates seven valuable principles from real-life stories to help readers reach their full potential. It's a must-read for students, businesspeople and all those who consider themselves underdogs."

—Joe Burrello

Head of Global Trading – IronBridge Capital Management
Assistant Football Coach – Glenbard West High School

"*The Wisdom of Walk-Ons* features three great narratives about overcoming adversity and succeeding both on and off the field. Corona builds on these inspirational stories by uncovering sound strategies we all can use. *The WoW* gave me an opportunity to reflect on my own 'walk-on' moments in life and ready myself for the next challenge."

—Geoffrey Phillips

Vice President and General Manager of Service Delivery
GATX Corporation

"Inspirational, motivational, and unimaginable! *The Wisdom of Walk-Ons* brilliantly correlates the trials and tribulations of walk-on athletes with those we face in business and life, and it more importantly provides the key strategies for overcoming them. *The WoW* is a must-read for any athlete, sports fan, college student, or businessperson. If you ever feel like giving up, apply it and you will succeed!"

—Joseph Dougherty, Jr.

Co-Founder and President
IPR, Inc.

"A great read! I found the anecdotes, messages and guidance as applicable and actionable for my 15-year-old son as they are for our sales team members with 15 years of experience."

—Jim Malpede

Vice President of Sales
Concur Technologies, Inc.

"Today's fiercely competitive business environment demands and rewards characteristics found in *The Wisdom of Walk-Ons*. With this easy-to-follow and actionable road map, Dr. Corona delivers powerful insights designed to bring out the 'walk-on' in all of us. Put these winning strategies to work in your life, and you'll see a path to realize your full potential."

—William Wilt, Jr.

Account Director – Sports Marketing
Goodby, Silverstein & Partners

"If you've ever faced doubters or been told you can't live your dream, you'll find *The WoW* a true testament to the 'I can, and I will' spirit that lies within all of us. Dr. Corona identifies seven practical success strategies in three fantastic but true stories about underdogs. This extraordinary book makes me want to yell, 'Put me in, Coach!'"

—Greg Farrall

All Big Ten Defense End – Indiana University, 1991
President and CEO – Farrall Wealth

For anyone who has ever felt like an underdog . . .

CONTENTS

Foreword by Bobby Bowden   1

Introduction to *The Wisdom of Walk-Ons*   3

Gordon Adams, corporate executive
    Southern California Trojans
    coached by John Robinson
    "You will never play at USC"   5

Alan Pizzitola, entrepreneur
    Alabama Crimson Tide
    coached by Paul "Bear" Bryant
    "Coach Bryant wants to see
    what you're made of"   33

Bob Bleyer, community business leader
    Notre Dame Fighting Irish
    coached by Dan Devine
    "Your application for admission
    to Notre Dame has been denied"   61

Their winning strategies   83

   1. Leverage your strengths   84

   2. Set stretch goals   87

   3. Work hard   89

   4. Stay balanced   92

   5. Be healthy   95

   6. Appreciate your supporters   98

   7. Help others succeed   101

Your game plan   105

   Step 1: Summarizing what you learned   106

   Step 2: Taking action   108

   Step 3: Tracking results   110

   Step 4: Telling your story   110

Speaking engagements, workshops,
  and coaching sessions   111

References   113

Acknowledgements   117

About the author   121

FOREWORD

*The second-winningest coach
in major college football history*

I've always said walk-ons are my favorite players. They love football so much that they play it for almost nothing in return. Most of them just work their tails off to help their teammates and coaches win football games; others become starters at their positions. Either way, I can tell you that walk-ons win big in the game of life.

Several of my former walk-on players from Florida State and West Virginia have succeeded in business and other kinds of careers. They've done well in their personal lives too. Much of this success is due to their integrity and drive. I believe a great deal of it also comes from what they learned as student-athletes in college.

Walk-ons are great examples of success because of *what* they do and *how* they do it. Paul Corona tells you all about it in *The Wisdom of Walk-Ons: 7 Winning Strategies for College, Business and Life*. I'll tell you, I haven't seen another book like it. I believe anyone can apply this wisdom and get better at work, at home, and in school.

You know, I still give talks across the country almost every week, and I love to tell good stories because people love to listen and learn from them. That's why I really like this book. It brings three amazing and *true* stories to life. You can't help but be inspired and motivated after reading them. Paul also spells out seven valuable lessons we all can learn from these great stories—and at the end he includes an action plan to help us apply the lessons in our own lives.

I wish you great success with *The WoW*!

Bobby Bowden
Tallahassee, Florida

INTRODUCTION TO
THE WISDOM OF WALK-ONS

wisdom [wiz-*duh* m]

—noun

the quality or state of being wise; knowledge of what is true or right coupled with just judgment as to action; sagacity, discernment, or insight.

walk-on [wawk-on, -awn]

—noun

an athlete trying out for a team who has not been drafted, specifically invited, scouted, awarded a scholarship, etc.

The Wisdom of Walk-Ons tells the true stories of three unheralded and unrecruited college football players who—against overwhelming odds—played for some of the greatest programs and Hall of Fame coaches in history: the Alabama Crimson Tide with Paul "Bear" Bryant, the Notre Dame Fighting Irish with Dan Devine, and the Southern California Trojans with John Robinson.

Former walk-ons Gordon Adams, Bob Bleyer, and Alan Pizzitola graduated from these storied universities in the 1970s and '80s with academic honors, national championship rings, practical skills, and a collection of winning strategies that helped them persevere and succeed in business and life in their 20s, 30s, 40s, and 50s. Fortunately, in 2010, they took time to put their feet up, reflect on their extraordinary experiences, and share their fantastic stories and priceless lessons with all of us.

Part inspiration and part self-improvement, *The Wisdom of Walk-Ons* combines the passion and pageantry of major college football, the inevitable ups and downs of business ambition, and a healthy perspective on what's ultimately important in life. It helps businesspeople, sports fans, current and former athletes—and all those who want more out of their professional and personal lives—become more successful and fulfilled.

I hope you enjoy reading *The WoW* and, more important, putting it to good use!

Paul L. Corona, MBA, EdD
Optimus Coaching
Chicago, Illinois

GORDON ADAMS
CORPORATE EXECUTIVE

*Southern California Trojans
coached by John Robinson*

"You will never play at USC"

GENETICALLY PREDISPOSED TROJAN

With junior quarterback Gordon Adams at the helm, the Newport Harbor Sailors reached the quarterfinals of the California high school playoffs in 1974. Despite higher expectations the following year, the team underachieved badly, posting a losing record and missing the postseason altogether. Gordon's average performance that year garnered him no interest from Division I college programs. His few suitors came from the Ivy League: the Harvard Crimson, the Yale Bulldogs, and the Dartmouth Big Green. While fleeting visions of Ivy success danced in his head, Gordon's Southern California Trojan pedigree tugged at his heart. His grandfather, parents, aunt, uncle, and four other relatives made him potentially the tenth family member in three generations to matriculate at USC, which he did in the fall of 1976.

Gordon knew his probability of success as a walk-on quarterback at a perennial college football powerhouse would be next to nil. Nevertheless, he convinced the man in the mirror to try by simply saying, "I'll never know if I don't give it a shot." The opportunity to get a great education at USC made walking on a nothing-to-lose bonus. Gordon's initial expectation was simultaneously ambitious and modest: just try to make the team. If that didn't happen, he reasoned, life would go on.

INAUSPICIOUS BEGINNINGS WITH A DYNASTY

By almost any measure, the USC football program, which played its first game in 1888, holds an enviable position among the nation's elite. Consider these accomplishments: 11 national championships, 31 bowl victories, 6 Heisman Trophy winners, 158 first-team All Americans, and 446 NFL players (and counting).

College Football Hall of Famer John McKay served as USC's head coach from 1960 to 1975. In 16 seasons with the Trojans, he won nine conference titles, five Rose Bowls, and four national championships. His successor, John Robinson, ended up winning three more conference titles, three more Rose Bowls, and another national championship before leaving to coach the Los Angeles Rams to two NFC championship games, losing both times to the eventual Super Bowl champions. Robinson also coached with Pro Football Hall of Famer John Madden as a member of the Oakland Raiders staff. In 2009, Coach Robinson joined Coach McKay in the College Football Hall of Fame.

Robinson took over the Trojans in 1976, the same year Gordon wanted to walk on. The assertive freshman's initial attempts at getting a preseason meeting with the new head coach proved fruitless, as repeated phone calls went unanswered. Finally, thanks to the intervention of a mutual contact, a call-back came. The aspiring quarterback found himself in the office of the future luminary, who did not mince words: "I can tell you right now that you're welcome to come out for the team, but you'll never play."

Undeterred, Gordon showed up for tryouts that fall. Different Trojan coaches greeted him with a polite but firm and surprising response: "The team for this season is already set. Walk-on tryouts for *next* season will be held in the spring. If you want, you can come back then." With that door slammed, Gordon the quarterback hopeful became just a mainstream USC freshman, going to class, hitting the library, building new friendships, and acclimating himself to college life in Los Angeles.

Informal "winter ball" gave interested players an opportunity to ready themselves for spring practice by lifting weights, running agility drills, and throwing passes. That winter of '77, the team roster featured *eight* scholarship quarterbacks and *zero* walk-on quarterbacks. Gordon jokes: "When I first arrived, I was ninth on a depth chart of eight." But after only his first workout with this select group, he believed that he could eventually compete with them.

Unfortunately, after only one week of spring practice, the decision makers disagreed. Tight-ends coach Norv Turner called Gordon into his office: "We've been watching you, Adams, and we think you have a fair amount of talent. But look who's in front of you. You're never going to play here. The good news is we have lots of friends who coach at smaller programs like Utah State, for example. With a phone call or two, we could probably get you into one of those schools, where you might get a chance to play. Are you interested?"

"Thanks, Coach. But I'm here first and foremost to get an education, and then to give football a shot. If I make the team, great. If not, then I'm at USC, and this is where I want to go to school."

That candid meeting with Norv Turner—who went on to become offensive coordinator of the Super Bowl Champion Dallas Cowboys, and then head coach of the Washington Redskins, Oakland Raiders, and San Diego Chargers—ironically boosted Gordon's confidence and validated his belief that he had what it took to compete at the Division I level. It's important to note, however, that the Trojan coaches were under no obligation whatsoever to give Gordon—or any walk-on—a closer look, an opportunity to attend meetings, or a chance to practice with the team. Coaches made commitments only to their scholarship players, who were promised an opportunity to participate in team activities and compete for playing time.

The next week, quarterbacks coach Paul Hackett—

who later coached future Pro Football Hall of Fame quarterback Joe Montana as a member of Bill Walsh's Super Bowl Champion San Francisco 49ers staff—sat Gordon down for a gut punch: "Look, I want to make sure one thing is perfectly clear. You will never play at USC. You might get a chance to practice a little bit and help the other guys get better. But I want to make sure you understand the reality you're facing. We recruit the very best players in the country, and they come here on scholarship. So I don't want you to have any misconceptions about what's going on, because *you will never play at USC*."

Not knowing how to respond, the resilient dreamer simply blurted out, "Okay. I got it, Coach. I understand my role."

A WISE PLAN: LEVERAGE STRENGTHS, WORK HARD, HELP OTHERS, AND BE PATIENT

Gordon Adams approached his walk-on challenge with realistic expectations and a wise plan. He knew that new head coach John Robinson and new quarterbacks coach Paul Hackett had heavily recruited another freshman quarterback, Paul McDonald (who later became an All American at USC and a starter for the Cleveland Browns). Any observer with a pulse could tell that Robinson and Hackett were grooming

McDonald to be their future starter, and that a walk-on had no chance of beating him out.

Gordon determined that the best way to get on the field after McDonald graduated was to stay on the team for four seasons (including a fifth year in school), master the Trojans' complex playbook, devour game film, and be an extraordinary teammate. In other words, Gordon planned to differentiate himself from the other "quarterbacks in waiting" by developing a deep knowledge of the game and demonstrating a positive attitude about his behind-the-scenes role. Those mental and emotional strengths, Gordon thought, could eventually be just as valuable as the more obvious physical strengths that the scholarship quarterbacks possessed in spades. "I was lucky enough to have a good mind for the game," he says, "so I knew my strength as a player would come from understanding offenses and defenses as well or better than anyone else on the field."

Gordon also decided not to worry about the older players above him on the depth chart. He instead focused on trying to be better than the younger ones who came in after him. That ultimately meant working harder and smarter, doing whatever the coaches asked, helping older and more talented teammates succeed, and patiently waiting for his chance to materialize during a fifth-year-senior season, when Paul McDonald would be gone.

Gordon left no stone unturned by being a good student, eating right, training hard, studying more film than the required amount, and going above and beyond the call of duty whenever an opportunity to contribute emerged. Perhaps most important, during practice and at games, he didn't just observe the action like an attentive fan on the edge of his seat. Gordon actively studied the field situation and the quarterback as if he were actually *playing* quarterback. He engaged in a continuous solitary game of "What would I do on this play if I were in there?" Thanks to these countless mental repetitions, Gordon developed an excellent understanding of Trojan football strategy. He could correctly read opposing defenses. He knew the right offensive plays to call. He could make split-second adjustments that might mean the difference between victory and defeat. In short, Gordon Adams became *good* at the physical side of football during his three years on the sidelines (1977, '78, and '79); he developed *greatness* in the mental aspects of the game, and that's how he planned to eventually separate himself from the pack in 1980.

SOPHOMORE WINS IT ALL BUT ANTICIPATES PRESSURE FROM BELOW

When spring practice ended before the start of Gordon's second season, only four quarterbacks remained in the running for the role of backup to Paul McDonald. Surprising sophomore Gordon Adams, who originally held the ninth spot on the depth chart, was in the hunt. What had happened to the other four? Three moved to different positions; the previous year's starter, Rob Hertel, had graduated and joined the Cincinnati Bengals.

Joining this select group of high potentials kept Gordon highly confident and motivated. While at USC, Hertel had treated Gordon well and boosted his confidence ("You're good enough to compete here, and don't let anyone tell you that you can't."). Gordon leaned on Hertel's endorsement when the coaches issued a reality check that fall before the first game of the year. They told Gordon he was doing well, but two guys on scholarship would get the opportunity to be McDonald's backup. That meant a fourth scholarship player and Gordon would hold the bottom spots on the depth chart and be extreme long shots to see any game action.

As that '78 season ended, and the 12-1 Trojans grasped two of the most coveted rings in college football—one for winning the Rose Bowl (USC's 16th) and another for winning the national championship (USC's 9th)—Gordon's celebration shrouded a potentially ominous reality: The pack of backup quarterbacks would grow bigger and hungrier the following year. Four high school All Americans (from California, New Jersey, Oklahoma, and Washington) had accepted scholarship offers from Coaches Robinson and Hackett, further crowding the depth chart and threatening Gordon's long-term goal to play as a fifth-year senior.

JUNIOR GETS BIG BREAK IN PALO ALTO AND PLEASANT SURPRISE IN LOS ANGELES

During year three, Gordon had "clearly the best day of my career" (he now jokes) when a heavily recruited high school All American quarterback named John Elway decided to sign with the Stanford Cardinal instead of USC. Elway, as fans know, starred for Stanford (consensus All American, Heisman Trophy runner-up, College Football Hall of Famer) and was later immortalized with the Denver Broncos (five Super Bowl starts, two Super Bowl championships, Pro Football Hall of Fame induction).

Just before training camp opened in the summer of '79, Gordon and the other Trojan quarterbacks were throwing the ball around when a man who hadn't said much to Gordon in previous years interrupted them. Coach Robinson pulled Gordon aside and spoke these magic words: "I want you to know that we appreciate the many good things you've done here, Gordon, and we have great respect for what you've accomplished so far. We believe that you can contribute even more in the future, so we're putting you on scholarship."

The door had finally opened. "I *knew* I had a shot to do something then," Gordon says, "because they wouldn't have awarded me a scholarship if they weren't serious about me competing for the backup job that year and the starting job the following year." Gordon's quietly confident call home that night ("Dad, I just earned a football scholarship to USC.") made his father beam with pride.

YET ANOTHER OBSTACLE TO OVERCOME

The second-class citizenship and the mountain climbing that characterized life as a walk-on didn't vanish simply because Gordon now sported a scholarship. A huge disappointment that season was not making the travel team, the select and smaller "team within the team" that went to away games. How did that happen? Typically, the first, the second, and sometimes the third players at each position traveled. In this case, Paul McDonald, Rob Preston (who later played for the Kansas City Chiefs and San Diego Chargers) and Scott Tinsley (a future Philadelphia Eagle) took their quarterback show on the road. Even though Gordon (not Tinsley) technically held the third spot on the QB depth chart, Tinsley was also the holder for field goals and extra points and, therefore, *had* to travel.

Coach Hackett broke the bad news: "I'm going to be honest with you, Gordon. This really sucks. You're important to this team. We think you're going to have a great opportunity to compete for the starting job next year. But you're not going to be able to travel this year."

"That really pissed me off," Gordon says. "I can remember thinking it wasn't fair, because I was on scholarship. I had earned the right to travel. But there I was, still a half step behind the *real* scholarship guys. It felt like I was *still* a walk-on. But it was my reality, another gut punch, and I had to deal with it. It just made me more motivated to earn the starting job the following year."

Gordon's father had prepared him for days like these, life experiences like these: "My dad always said, 'Whatever you do, do your best, do it right, do it to the fullest, and don't quit.' I followed his advice then, and I still apply it today."

Gordon's retrospective on what happened then

gives anyone who faces challenges and temporary disappointments wise words to live by: "If you work hard, do the right things, and have confidence, you'll eventually get your opportunity. And when it comes, you'd better be prepared to take advantage of it. You have to simultaneously be patient and maintain an inner drive to be the best you can be."

SURROUNDED BY GREATNESS

Clearly, most of Gordon Adams's resilience came from his extraordinary inner drive. He's quick to admit, though, that another key piece of the puzzle came from his inspirational surroundings: "I knew every day as a Trojan football player that I was very fortunate to be a part of greatness—and it was fun. Winning two Rose Bowls and a national championship, finishing No. 2 in the country another year, seeing Charles White win the Heisman Trophy, and playing alongside so many outstanding football players who were also good people—that, in and of itself, was really special. And our coaching staff—John Robinson, Norv Turner, and Dave Wannstedt—became head coaches in the NFL. Our offensive line coach, Hudson Houck, ended up coaching offensive lines that blocked for some of the greatest running backs in the history of football: Charles White [won the Heisman Trophy, played for

the Cleveland Browns and the Los Angeles Rams],
Marcus Allen [won the Heisman Trophy, played for the
Los Angeles Raiders and the Kansas City Chiefs, won
the Super Bowl, in the Pro Football Hall of Fame],
Eric Dickerson [played for four NFL teams, in the
Pro Football Hall of Fame], Ricky Williams [won the
Heisman Trophy, played for the New Orleans Saints
and the Miami Dolphins], and Emmitt Smith [played
for the Dallas Cowboys and the Arizona Cardinals, won
three Super Bowls, in the Pro Football Hall of Fame].
All of these coaches were great guys who were really
competitive and intense. And Coach Robinson was
phenomenal at bringing all of them together, managing a huge set of healthy egos, and getting outstanding
results."

WINNING STRATEGIES CAN MAKE DREAMS COME TRUE

The Trojans closed the 1979 campaign (Gordon's
junior season) with their 17th Rose Bowl championship, a No. 2 national ranking, and their third Heisman
Trophy (won by tailback Charles White). After the
closing words and final applause ended the annual
team banquet a few weeks later, a few coaches caught
up with Gordon's parents before they reached the exit.
This ostensibly friendly goodbye to Mom and Dad

included a foretelling motivational message for their son: "Mr. and Mrs. Adams, we're expecting big things from Gordon next year." That good news gave Gordon a new surge of confidence. He felt that he had a real shot at accomplishing something truly fantastic: becoming the starting quarterback for the USC Trojans.

An intensely motivated Gordon showed up for spring practice before the start of his fifth-year-senior season. Then he and five other eager quarterbacks began the wide-open race to win the starting job. Standard procedure called for a preliminary assessment by the coaching staff after two weeks of competition so that an initial pecking order could be established. After each day, the self-assessment voice inside Gordon assured him that he had done well, that things were looking good.

At the two-week mark, Coach Hackett invited Gordon to lunch before their regular meeting with the rest of the quarterbacks. At the restaurant, Hackett sat across from Gordon at a private table, looked him in the eye, and said with a serious smile, "This shouldn't come as a surprise, Gordon: You've earned the opportunity to be the starting quarterback for the USC Trojans."

Thirty-one years later, the 52-year-old former walk-on remembered that moment with just the right combination of pride and humility, as if it happened yesterday: "That was one of those great days in life, when everything falls into place and the big reward comes for all the hard work. It was a dream come true."

LET THE GAMES BEGIN

The Trojans fielded one of the nation's best defenses in Gordon's senior year. It featured future NFL heavyweights Ronnie Lott (won four Super Bowls with the San Francisco 49ers, selected to the Pro Football Hall of Fame), Chip Banks (made All Pro with the Cleveland Browns), Joey Browner (made All Pro with the Minnesota Vikings), Dennis Smith (made All Pro with the Denver Broncos), Riki Ellison (won three Super Bowls with the San Francisco 49ers), and Jeff Fisher (won the Super Bowl with the Chicago Bears, has been an NFL head coach for 17 years running), among others.

The firepower on the other side of the ball came from a rock-solid offensive line that included Keith Van Horne (All American, won the Super Bowl with the Chicago Bears), Don Mosebar (made All Pro and won the Super Bowl with the Los Angeles Raiders), Bruce Mathews (made All Pro with the Tennessee Titans, in the Pro Football Hall of Fame)—and, as mentioned earlier, a tailback named Marcus Allen (won the

Heisman Trophy, played for the Los Angeles Raiders and the Kansas City Chiefs, won the Super Bowl, in the Pro Football Hall of Fame). Gordon's strong receivers included tight end Hoby Brenner (played for the New Orleans Saints).

Quarterbacks coach Paul Hackett talked candidly in his first summer-camp meeting with first-year starter Gordon Adams: "Let's look at how this season is likely to unfold. We're going to run the ball on first down. We're going to run the ball on second down. If it's third and short, we'll run again. If it's third and long, we'll pass. If we want to pass, and a receiver isn't wide open, throw the ball away. We'll punt and play stifling defense. Your job, Gordon, is to not [f***] things up."

Gordon replied with a reassuring smile and the correct answer: "Coach, I think I got it. I think I understand what I'm supposed to do."

Hackett continued, "If you make a bad play, just shake it off. And always remember, you don't have to *win* games for us; you just need to *manage* them. We'll have a good team this way."

OPENING NIGHT

For their first game of the 1980 season, the seventh-ranked Trojans traveled to Knoxville to take on the Tennessee Volunteers before a capacity crowd of 95,049 in always unfriendly and deafening Neyland Stadium. The night game, broadcast nationally on a new cable television station called ESPN, gave Gordon thrills and chills as he took the field and fulfilled every high school quarterback's fantasy of starting for the mighty USC Trojans.

With the game tied 17-17 and about two minutes remaining, USC cornerback Jeff Fisher intercepted a pass and put the game in the hands of the offense led by Gordon Adams, who was playing in the first full game of his college career. After driving close to field-goal range, the Trojans took a stupid penalty that moved them back to the Tennessee 45-yard line with only 10 seconds left. Gordon called timeout and hustled to the sideline to get the final play. With the game on the line, on national television, in a stadium so loud you couldn't hear yourself think, Coach Robinson looked at his petrified rookie quarterback and calmly said, "Isn't this great? This is what it's all about. We've got 10 seconds left, and we need to do something to win this game."

Gordon remembered that decisive moment of keeping calm under pressure as one of Coach Robinson's many great acts of leadership, along with recruiting talented coaches and players, bringing them together, uniting around a vision of success, and enjoying the experience (not just the accomplishment).

The inexperienced starter had delivered a good game to that point in terms of passing statistics and no turnovers. But now it all came down to one play; the Trojans needed a tough 15 yards to get into field-goal range. Gordon dropped back to pass and calmly hit his tight end, who got out of bounds for the 15-yard gain. Then the kicker, Eric Hipp, blocked out the chaos of the crowd, shifted the weight of the world from his shoulders to his leg, and nailed a 47-yard field goal to win the game as time ran out, stunning the Tennessee faithful into a sad, angry silence. In the middle of the pile of delirious Trojans, the walk-on had finally arrived.

ADAMS VS. ELWAY

As the season progressed, USC stacked victories and climbed the national polls. Then things didn't go as expected. After opening with five straight wins, the second-ranked Trojans laid an egg at Oregon, tying the Ducks 7-7. But Gordon and company recovered quickly the next week, blowing out the California Bears 60-7.

The eighth game of the season, on the road against Stanford, pitted former walk-on Gordon Adams against future legend John Elway, who ended up becoming one of the greatest quarterbacks in NFL history. That day the Chevrolet Player of the Game Award, on the ABC television network, went to one of those quarterbacks—the one from USC—who led his team to a convincing 34-9 victory, disappointing the sellout home crowd of 84,892.

A PIVOTAL PLAY

By pounding California and Stanford, the Trojans recaptured the No. 2 national ranking before heading home to the world-famous Los Angeles Memorial Coliseum—site of the 1932 (and later 1984) Summer Olympics, the 1959 World Series, and the 1967 and '73 Super Bowls, as well as former home of the LA Rams (and future home of the LA Raiders). USC expected to beat the unranked and outmatched Washington Huskies the afternoon of November 15, 1980. However, Murphy's Law attended the game, and Gordon suffered a season-ending knee injury on the last play of the first half. Adding insult to Gordon's injury, the underdog Huskies ended the Trojans' 28-game unbeaten streak with a 20-10 upset. With Gordon in a cast on the sidelines, USC lost its next game to UCLA and then beat Notre Dame to finish the season with an 8-2-1 record and a No. 11 ranking.

Gordon admits experiencing the negative thoughts and emotions of a storybook college career prematurely ended by injury—shock, disbelief, anger, and disappointment. But what emerged at season's end and remains to this day is the ultimate, overwhelmingly positive takeaway: He turned his fantasy into reality, starting at quarterback for the USC Trojans as a former walk-on, after being told by three future NFL coaches that he would never even play a down.

WORKING HARD AND STAYING BALANCED

As Gordon looks back on his college career, he mentions lessons he learned from others' examples, including the "work-hard-play-hard" rule. "I was lucky enough to be a member of a fraternity with some world-class swimmers," he says. "One was Bruce Furniss, who broke two world records and won two gold medals in the 1976 Montreal Olympics; he also ended up winning six NCAA titles. These guys had fun and enjoyed life. But when it was time to get in the pool, they were *all* business—working hard and being great. So I learned that I could have fun when it was time to have fun, but I had to really work hard when it was time to work."

It was a lesson that reinforced what his parents had already instilled in him about the value of hard work: "I came to college with a high degree of self-motivation. I knew I was at USC to get an education, first and foremost, and I wanted to get A's and learn as much as I could. I loved learning about my major, business."

Balanced success for many student-athletes on the Trojan football team resembled a high-wire act by the Flying Wallendas. As a backup quarterback during the season, Gordon was on the practice field, in meetings, in the film room or at team meals from about 12:30 to 6:30 p.m., Monday through Friday. All day Saturday was devoted to the game. The *starting* quarterback role was even more demanding. Morning classes ran from 8 to 11. Football activities began at 11:30 a.m., allowing for an extra hour of private meetings with the coaches. Team time on the practice field, in meetings, in the film room, or at meals still ran from 12:30 to 6:30 p.m. More film study after dinner lasted until 8—and then homework consumed what was left of the evening.

So how well did Gordon Adams balance the sometimes competing demands of being a student and an athlete? While building a remarkable career on the football field, he won the team award for highest cumulative grade point average among lettermen in both his junior and senior years, graduated with a 3.7 GPA, and earned Pac-10 All-Academic honors his senior year—posting the highest GPA in the conference.

A STRONG TEAM OF SUPPORTERS

Gordon still appreciates his supporters—particularly his parents—who early on instilled motivation, energy, and passion to succeed through the example they set, the guidance they provided, and the excellence they expected. The transition from high school to college gave Gordon a natural opportunity to move from his immediate family, which valued hard work and success, to the Trojan football family that expected the same things.

Strong mentors, such as John Robinson, provided the life-changing opportunity for Gordon to prove himself as a walk-on and earn a scholarship to USC. "I still have great respect for Coach Robinson and his leadership," Gordon says. Coach Hackett deserves a tremendous amount of credit for teaching Gordon to play quarterback, taking advantage of his strengths, and developing him into a starter: "I wouldn't have been able to achieve what I did without Paul Hackett."

Another key supporter and mentor—Paul Salata, a loyal USC alumnus, who played in the NFL and is now a generous philanthropist—gave Gordon an opportunity to work in his company after Gordon was cut by the Dallas Cowboys in the preseason of 1981. Serious fans of the NFL recognize Salata as the founder of an annual event called "Irrelevant Week," which benefits local charities and celebrates the success of underdogs by honoring "Mr. Irrelevant," the last player picked in the draft.

Gordon also credits his wife and partner, Anne, with playing a key role in any success he attained as an athlete and a business leader. When they started dating at USC, she kept him grounded through the great highs and occasional lows of quarterbacking the Trojans. Today, Gordon says the couple's healthy perspective on the inevitable ups and downs of business ambition and family life helps keep him balanced at work and home. Fall football Saturdays find Gordon, Anne, and their three daughters—Vanessa, Claire, and Ali, all USC alumnae—still cheering for the Trojans.

AFTER THE BAND STOPPED PLAYING: LEADERSHIP IN BUSINESS

In Gordon's business career of over 30 years, he has taken on increasingly demanding responsibilities at IBM, EDS, and Tyco International. He is currently senior vice president of sales and professional services for Tyco Retail Solutions, which offers electronic security products for retailers. He had been senior vice president of sales and marketing at radio frequency identification (RFID) infrastructure provider Vue Technology, now a part of Tyco. Before then he was vice president and regional manager for Affiliated Computer Services, a leader in informational technology outsourcing. Earlier in his career he worked for 17 years at Electronic Data Systems (EDS) in senior leadership roles in sales, marketing, and customer relations. Before joining EDS he spent over four years with IBM.

NATURAL STRENGTHS

Making the transition from quarterback on the field to quarterback in the office was "a perfect fit," Gordon says. For most of his career, Gordon's success has depended on the ability to assemble and unite diverse, talented teams to solve sophisticated business problems such as landing complex, multimillion-dollar, long-term contracts. He must utilize the strengths of all team members, letting them know why their contributions are vital and showing them sincere appreciation. "I believe that successful people figure out what they're naturally good at, and then they go out and make a living at that instead of trying to succeed at what someone else thinks they should be doing," Gordon notes.

What Gordon calls "starting with the reality check" extends beyond one's career choice. His business leadership decisions are guided by honest assessments of situations: "If it's a business deal we're pursuing, we have to start with: Can we compete? Do we have what it takes?"

OWNING SUCCESS AND FAILURE

Being realistic and taking responsibility go hand in hand. "As a quarterback, I learned to take responsibility for the entire offensive performance. Don't blame the receiver who drops a pass or the lineman who misses a block and I get sacked. Don't blame the refs. Take responsibility for your success or failure. This has such a huge application to business. We can always blame the boss or the competition, but we make our own fortune."

LIFE IS A TEAM SPORT

While taking responsibility for oneself, Gordon says, give credit to those not in the spotlight—those whose vital contributions may go underappreciated and unrecognized. It's a lesson he recalls Coach Hackett teaching the Trojan quarterbacks: No one person accomplishes anything significant without help; the supporting cast usually does most of the heavy lifting in football, business, and life's other endeavors. It follows that true leadership is not at all about helping *yourself* succeed but about helping *others* succeed.

Gordon says he applies the lessons of the gridiron to his life outside work too. For example, he coached his own daughters and their friends, imparting the lesson that sports success at the youth level is about learning new skills, experiencing good teamwork, building true friendships, and doing one's best in all situations. These key takeaways are remembered and applied long after won-loss records are forgotten.

He also keeps up the dedication to physical fitness that was required of him as a Trojan football player, which meant weight training, running, eating right, and getting rest. Competing interests make it easy for any working adult to get out of shape, but "you just feel better and perform better when you stay in shape," Gordon says. "If your mind and body are active, you'll be healthier and happier."

THE WISDOM OF A WALK-ON

The lesson that keeps Gordon honest and hungry is that sustained success requires habitual hard work, continuous learning, and perseverance. Walk-ons can't afford to let up when they're surrounded by eager scholarship players loaded with talent, just as businesspeople can't rest on their laurels in a competitive and dynamic marketplace.

Gordon's closing words about his valuable learning experiences in college say it all: "Dealing with the challenges and adversity of being a walk-on, and playing a high-visibility sport at USC, certainly helped prepare me well for life's challenges." Now we all can benefit from Gordon's inspirational story and its priceless lessons (and those of the other former walk-ons profiled in this book).

ALAN PIZZITOLA
ENTREPRENEUR

*Alabama Crimson Tide
coached by Paul "Bear" Bryant*

*"Coach Bryant wants to see
what you're made of"*

ROLLERCOASTER RIDE FROM BIRMINGHAM TO TUSCALOOSA

Alan Pizzitola's high school football program was so bad he quit playing after his sophomore year to focus on basketball. Then just before Alan's senior year (1971), a new head coach took over the John Carroll Catholic Cavaliers of Birmingham, Alabama, and talked Alan into coming out of early retirement. Alan wondered if he had done the right thing after the team started the season with two losses. Seven straight victories later, his doubts were removed.

Despite Alan's earning All Metro honors at season's end, coaches from the University of Alabama weren't paying attention to his play at strong safety. They were focused on the Cavaliers' star tailback, for whom Alan blocked as a fullback. The Crimson Tide, already loaded with blue-chip scholarship recruits at tailback that year, ended up offering the Cavaliers' tailback only an opportunity to try out for the team as an invited walk-on. That sounded pretty good to him, but he also wanted his good buddy Alan Pizzitola to come along for the long hard ride: "C'mon, man, do this with me," he pleaded. Alan just laughed at the absurdity of the idea. He couldn't even *imagine* himself playing in Tuscaloosa for the Tide and legendary head coach Paul "Bear" Bryant—until he mentioned it to his father, who calmly said, "Why not?"

"My dad's response shocked me," Alan remembered 32 years later as if it happened yesterday. "Dad, it's *Alabama*. What makes you think I can compete at that level? I'm barely getting looked at by Division II schools."

"You got better and better with every game this year," his father replied confidently. You'll never know unless you try. What have you got to lose?"

After sleeping on the ostensibly crazy idea, the son admitted to himself that Dad might actually be right. After all, Alan had been admitted by Alabama as a student and had already decided to attend, so he really didn't have anything to lose by trying.

With the confidence and excitement that a proud and caring father can inspire in a son, Alan ran to tell his high school coach the next day about his plan to walk on at Alabama. The coach responded by laughing out loud.

Undaunted and even a bit defiant, Alan called the Alabama football office to find out what he needed to do to walk on that summer with his good buddy the tailback. A few weeks later, with proper paperwork on file in the university's athletic department—and his summer conditioning schedule in hand—the real fun began for this overlooked strong safety.

WHAT I DID DURING MY SUMMER VACATION

Every morning at 6 a.m. and every night at 5 p.m., Alan (the future *uninvited* walk-on) and his good buddy, the great tailback (the future *invited* walk-on) trained and pushed each other harder and harder. They had a common difficult goal: to arrive at summer practice in Tuscaloosa in top physical condition, able to pass every test the Crimson Tide coaches threw at them and the other players (scholarship and nonscholarship, upperclassmen and underclassmen). A daily regimen of endurance running, wind sprints, and weight lifting—for hours in the stifling humidity and scorching summer heat of the Deep South—made for a pretty challenging summer vacation.

Finally, the last day of partner training arrived for these two Cavalier alumni, who had accomplished their first goal of getting in great shape. Beaming with confidence and anticipation, they agreed to drive separately to Tuscaloosa the next morning in time for the opening of summer practice with the Crimson Tide and the start of college life. Then a funny thing happened: Alan's good buddy, the star tailback, didn't show.

EARLY OBSTACLES ON CAMPUS

Without his tailback companion, Alan felt like an imposter trying out for the revered Tide team of over 125 proven players. Less confident, and clearly uninvited, he thought to himself, "I've walked into a foreign country, and I can't even understand the language." The piercing eyes of the other players and the coaches said loudly and in unison, "What are *you* doing here?" Alan's check-in phone call home that night was brief and to the point: "Dad, I'm coming home; I have no buddy here to help me through this."

In fact, "no buddy" and "nobody" were literally one and the same for Alan as he moved into his freshman dorm room. While all the other "real" players lived large in plush Paul Bryant Hall (the athletes' dorm), Alan the walk-on lived by himself, on the other end of campus, in the oldest dorm available; University officials had dutifully opened a room early for him.

"I was really feeling sorry for myself. I was angry at my buddy who didn't show. I was mad at my dad for talking me into trying out. I was mad at the world. If my dad had said when I called him that first night, 'Okay, come home,' I would have. But he didn't, so I stayed. And I made up my mind that if I threw my hat in the ring, then this early adversity wasn't going to make me pick it up."

The deck seemed to be stacked against Alan and the other walk-ons: "A real problem from the start was, No. 1, I was a walk-on; No. 2, I was an *uninvited* walk-on; No. 3, there were all kinds of other players also trying to walk on. As a group, we were looked at by the coaching staff with at least a question mark about who would get hurt because this was big-time football. And at that time, Division I programs could sign 45 scholarship players each year. So even getting noticed as a walk-on, with that many scholarship guys on the field, was a high hurdle to clear."

So Alan naturally became part of the "out crowd" of walk-ons, in contrast to the "in crowd" of scholarship players. Of course, being part of the out crowd did not bode well for getting in the game, figuratively or literally. But Alan made up his mind to treat this early obstacle as a challenge to overcome: "As a walk-on, walls are all around you, and you need to climb each one to eventually succeed."

Merely getting dressed was difficult at first. Alan and the other walk-ons received their gear (helmet, pads, shoes, and practice uniform) from the skeptical equipment manager after all the scholarship players had been outfitted to the nines. Scholarship players got shiny new stuff right out of the box; it smelled factory fresh and looked cool. Walk-ons got the equivalent of hand-me-downs off a dusty shelf; their garb smelled like an old locker room and looked rejected. "My shoes were too big, and my shoulder pads were *really* too big," Alan recalls. After a few days of practice, a concerned coach finally noticed and said, "Where did you get those shoulder pads, son? They're too big. Get them off before you get hurt, and go get yourself some that fit." Armed with the clout of a coach's order, Alan revisited the equipment manager, who magically found him a new pair of properly fitting shoulder pads and a new pair of shoes to boot. (This equipment manager who gave Alan a hard time early on became a good friend later.)

WELCOME TO BIG-TIME COLLEGE FOOTBALL

On the first day of practice in full pads, the Crimson Tide defense played a neat little game called "Bull in the Ring." The ring consisted of about 20 hungry linebackers and defensive backs waiting anxiously in a circle while one randomly chosen player jumped into the center for his turn to knock their blocks off. At the sound of the coach's whistle, the "bull" went wild (like when the restraining gate pops open in a rodeo) and charged at his teammates. They charged back. A better name for this game would have been "Head-On Collision." Coaches introduce these kinds of practice drills to get an idea of who's tough and who's soft, who's a gamer and who's a quitter. They're really fun for players who are strong, aggressive, and half-crazy. Alan was fairly strong and aggressive for an 18-year-old freshman, but he wasn't the least bit crazy. The call home that night: "Dad, I'm telling you, these guys are really nuts. I've made a big mistake coming here."

During the all-important 40-yard-dash test the following day, Alan ran a 5.0. The time was slow as molasses for a defensive back in the Southeastern Conference in the early 1970s and would be beyond laughable today. This bad result earned Alan a visit from another puzzled coach.

"Where did you learn how to run, son?"

"What do you mean, Coach?"

"I mean, WHO TAUGHT YOU HOW TO RUN?"

"Well, no one did."

"OBVIOUSLY! Do you realize that there's a correct way to run?"

Alan didn't answer.

"You're swinging your arms across your body and shifting your weight all wrong. You're preventing yourself from being fast. You need to learn how to run, Pizzitola."

So the 'Bama coaches (who must have seen some potential in this walk-on) began teaching Alan how to run like the major college football players who surrounded him. By the end of his first season, Alan's 40-time had dropped to an impressive 4.65.

The coaches eventually did another thing that made all the difference in the world for Alan. They gave him sight—they literally helped him see well enough to play at the Division I level.

First, a little background about why keen eyesight matters: Defensive backs rely heavily on their "reads," not just on pure strength and speed. They read opposing offensive players by watching (and reacting to) their body movements, which tip the defenders off to what's coming. For example, quarterbacks tend to look in the direction they're going to pass one or two seconds before releasing the ball. By reading the quarterback's face, a defensive back can anticipate the intended receiver of a pass and then make a better play on the ball. A defensive back first depends on his eyes and brain to put himself in the right position to then use his arms and legs. Good instincts and split-second reactions separate starters from reserves and can mean the difference between victory and defeat.

One day during practice, the defensive backs coach got all over Alan for not making a quick enough break on the quarterback's pass: "Pizzitola, you've got to read and react faster than that! When you see the quarterback's eyes lock on the strong-side receiver, start leaning that way so you get a good jump on the ball before it's released."

Honestly puzzled by his coach's suggestion, Alan replied, "You can see the quarterback's eyes from here?"

"What?" countered the coach.

"Can you see the quarterback's eyes from back here? I can't."

"Do you ever wear glasses?"

"Just for driving and seeing long distances."

"When was your last eye test?"

"I don't remember."

"Talk to the head trainer after practice. Get your eyes checked, and get yourself some contact lenses—right away."

The next day, with new contact lenses on his eyeballs and more spring in his step, Alan felt like a new man on the football field. He could see which way the quarterback was looking. He could see the ball as soon as it left the quarterback's hand. And with this new clear vision, Alan's reading and reaction times improved dramatically. Soon he became known as a player with "a nose for the ball," a guy who seemed to anticipate faster than many of his teammates where the play was going. The tide gradually turned throughout his freshman year from self-doubt to growing confidence as Alan's performance improvements began adding up. He was becoming a legitimate Division I player.

TRUE STUDENT-ATHLETE

Alan's success off the field, in the classroom, also helped him move from the outer circle to the inner circle. A few teammates and he took some of the same business courses. The other players wouldn't sit with Alan in class because they were on scholarship and he was a walk-on—but they did speak to him, particularly after class one day when the professor handed back their first exam. The scores of these scholarship players reflected some underperformance.

"What did you get, Pizzitola?"

"98."

"98? You're smart?"

"I usually do well in school."

"Then can we study with you?"

"Sure."

Soon, Alan the Tutor received regular invitations from the scholarship players to study with them in Paul Bryant Hall. The more he helped them with their schoolwork, the more they accepted him in the locker room and on the field.

OPPORTUNITY MEETS PREPARATION

A few weeks into summer camp of that first season, two strong safeties on the varsity went down with serious injuries, forcing the coaches to reluctantly pull up a couple of scholarship players from the freshmen squad. This gave Alan an unexpected opportunity to get some serious practice time on the freshmen squad (and more exposure to the coaches). Then during the first live scrimmage, the strong safety ahead of Alan went down with an injury, which caused the defensive backs coach to study his clipboard and find out whose name came up next on the depth chart. Alan recalled this frustrated coach's body language and voice, both of which yelled, "WHO IS PIZZITOLA?"

"I am, sir."

"Do you know what you're doing, son?"

"Yes, sir."

"Then get in there."

Even as an 18-year-old freshman walk-on, Alan already knew he always had to be prepared—he always had to be ready to go—in case his number got called. And he sure was ready on this occasion. He jumped right in and made the tackle on the next four plays. The defensive backs coach blew his whistle to stop play, walked over to Alan and said, "Who are you, again, and where are you from?"

"Alan Pizzitola, sir, from Birmingham."

From that day forward, Alan Pizzitola stayed on the radar of his freshmen teammates and coaches, who tested him more and more with additional playing time during live scrimmages. By the freshmen team's opening game, Alan the walk-on had earned himself a job as the starting strong safety. Little by little, his performance had improved. After only one month in Tuscaloosa, Alan had transformed his initial self-doubt and negative self-talk into growing self-confidence and positive expectations.

The Crimson Tide freshmen opened their season by falling to the Ramblin' Wreck from George Tech 14-0. Game 2, against the Vanderbilt Commodores, started with the offense struggling again and the whole team in need of a spark. From his strong safety position, Alan read the opposing quarterback's moves and then saw his eyes lock on an intended receiver. After Alan intercepted the pass and returned it for a touchdown, the Freshmen Tide's first points of the year, his coaches *really* began to pay him some serious attention. With each game came more improvement, stronger performance, and greater confidence. By season's end, Alan just knew he belonged, so he made an appointment to talk with Coach Bryant.

THE BIG ASK

Alan had a dual purpose in meeting with the most revered coach in college football: to let Bryant know he had made a mistake by not recruiting him out of high school (because in Alan's mind, he was the best freshman strong safety on the team) and to convince him to put Alan on scholarship. Always prepared, Alan had rehearsed hard with his father, who played the role of devil's advocate. If Alan said this, his father said that. If Alan proposed one thing, his dad countered with another. They covered every possible scenario they could think of to make sure the walk-on would leave the head coach's office with the well-deserved scholarship.

After confidently knocking on the big oak door, Alan heard an indifferent voice say, "Come in."

"Hello, Coach Bryant, I'm Alan Pizzitola."

The Legend peered over reading glasses that rested at the end of his nose and replied in a slightly annoyed tone: "I know who you are. Sit down."

Coach Bryant actually had no guest chairs in his office, only a long, old, soft couch into which wide-eyed intimidated visitors sank while he looked down at them from the throne behind his oversized desk.

The walk-on freshman's self-confidence and certainty of purpose evaporated quickly while he waited silently for what seemed like an eternity. Coach Bryant evidently had important paperwork to finish before entertaining his now-anxious guest.

An emotionless "Can I help you?" came out of the coach's mouth as he looked up, removed his glasses, and held them in one hand.

"Yes, sir. I played freshmen ball this season, and—quite honestly—I'm as good as anyone you recruited last year. I believe I deserve a scholarship, and I'd like to talk to you about . . ."

Up shot Coach Bryant's other hand: "Stop! *Nobody* gets a scholarship at the University of Alabama for playing freshmen football. You bring your little [a**] out here for spring ball with the varsity, and we'll find out what you're made of then."

Shocked, Alan had no rebuttal. He and his dad hadn't thought of that one.

"Yes, sir. Thank you, sir."

As this less-than-a-minute discussion concluded, Alan scampered out of Bear Bryant's office like a little puppy dog with his tail between his legs.

SPRING PRACTICE AS SPRINGBOARD

When spring practice finally started, Alan found himself listed on the varsity depth chart as the lowly fifth-string strong safety. Only two weeks later, just before the second live scrimmage, his increasingly strong performance had rocketed him to second string. But in his heart, Alan believed he should have been first. To support his conviction with compelling evidence, he had nothing less than a career day during that scrimmage. He knocked down two passes. He blitzed and sacked the quarterback. He made seven tackles. Everything just came together beautifully and, he felt, it should have been painfully obvious to all the players and coaches on hand that their new starting strong safety was Alan Pizzitola.

The next day, eager Alan checked the depth chart before practice, expecting to finally see his name in its rightful position, first. But instead it appeared fifth.

After a flawless, standout performance as the second stringer the day before, Alan not only hadn't risen to first string, he had inexplicably dropped to fifth.

As Alan—now a 56-year-old, good-humored family man and businessperson—vividly recalled this 37-year-old collegiate injustice, his face and voice transformed into those of the enraged 19-year-old he was that day: "I was really pissed off. *I can't tell you* how angry I was."

Please hold that thought for a minute . . .

College football lore tells us that Bear Bryant used to coach practice from an observation tower; Alan vouches for it. Perched high in the sky, the great coach could see the entire team at once and zero in on individual players as needed. A bullhorn made his deep southern drawl sound as if God was actually barking orders from the clouds. Wise Coach Bryant always customized his leadership approach to fit the different motivational needs of individual players. For example, sometimes he would swoop down from his tower like an eagle eyeing easy prey, grab a lazy or careless player's face mask, and light him up with "encouragement." On other occasions, for self-motivated players who needed another kind of feedback, he would offer insightful commentary without leaving the tower. One time, Alan let an easy interception slip right through his hands. "Nice hands, Pizzitola" is all God said (and all he had to say). Alan didn't miss another pass for a month.

Now back to the part about dropping from second team to fifth after having a career day and expecting to be moved up to first . . .

Alan phoned home with the bad news and a warning: "Dad, this could be it. I've had enough. They really don't want me here. If something good doesn't happen at practice this afternoon, I'll probably quit. I'm sorry, but I can't take this emotional rollercoaster any more. It's just not worth it."

An extremely peeved Alan took the practice field with a scowl on his face and a chip on his shoulder, and he started going through the motions in an obviously uncharacteristic manner. About half an hour passed before linebackers coach Pat Dye (who later became Auburn's head coach and a member of the College Football Hall of Fame) put his arm around Alan and said, "What's your problem?"

"*You know* what my problem is. Nobody out here was better than me yesterday, and I went from second team down to fifth. That's just not right. If y'all don't want me here, just tell me."

Coach Dye kept one arm around Alan, looked him right in the eye, pointed at Coach Bryant's tower with the other hand, and said, "You see that man in the tower? He knows better than anyone out here that you were the best yesterday. Today, he wants to find out what you do when things don't go your way. *Coach Bryant wants to see what you're made of* . . . He's watching every move you make, Alan. And right now, you're letting yourself down."

Oh, that really got Alan's goat. He thought to himself, "Okay, if that's the way it's going to be, I can win this mind game. Now they'll really see what I'm made of." During the next live scrimmage against the first-team offense, Alan hit 'Bama's starting tight end so hard on a crossing pattern that he knocked himself and the tight end out cold. Another day, he repeatedly hammered future NFL quarterback Richard Todd, who—after the third time—finally jumped up and screamed at Alan, "WHO IN THE [H***] ARE *YOU*?" and then at his offensive line, "CAN *SOMEBODY* BLOCK THIS WALK-ON?"

At the conclusion of the spring practice season, the Crimson Tide coaches voted "this walk-on" the hardest hitter on the team, for which Alan won the Lee Roy Jordan Headhunter Award. Then before the beginning of summer camp, Coach Bryant awarded Alan Pizzitola an athletic scholarship.

SHIFTING INTO HIGH GEAR

With that scholarship in hand and a new lease on life, Alan's goal stretched from just making the team to eventually becoming the starting strong safety. In his sophomore season (1973) Alan happily played second string behind David McMakin, a senior who mentored him well. During practice one Monday afternoon, Alan lined up for a play with the starters while McMakin observed them from behind like a coach: "Alan, with this formation, they'll run a sweep to the left. Look for it."

Sure enough, the quarterback pitched the ball to the running back, who went left as the offensive line led the way on a sweep. After making the tackle (and feeling a little like a cheater with inside information), Alan asked his mentor, "How did you know it would happen just like that?"

"I was in the film room studying formations and plays last night."

"On a Sunday night, you were in the film room? Today's only Monday; we have all week to prepare."

"I start preparing every Sunday night."

From that moment on, Alan knew that while he certainly wasn't the best athlete on the team, he could outwork anybody on preparation. By studying film of

Alabama's opponents, learning their tendencies, reading formations, and anticipating plays—the often underappreciated strategic aspects of football—Alan capitalized on his strong intellect.

McMakin the starter and Alan the backup made key contributions to the Crimson Tide that magical season and were rewarded with Alabama's ninth national championship.

LEADERSHIP ON AND OFF THE FIELD

One year later—as the junior starting strong safety—Alan was picked to call all the defensive signals, had authority to change plays that the coaches sent in, and became one of the leading brains of the Crimson Tide defense. Another good thing happened to Alan the *student*-athlete during his junior year. His love of math (in this case, a statistics course), his diligence in study hall, and a stretch request from his mother all came together just right. Alan had already earned high grades most semesters, but his mom knew he was capable of more: "Why do you stop yourself short in the classroom, Alan?"

"What do you mean?

"I'd like to see you make the dean's list—just once."

So for the fall semester—during football season—Alan worked even harder on his schoolwork and then brought his mom one of her most cherished Christmas presents ever, a 3.5 (dean's list) report card from the University of Alabama. By the end of the school year, he added Academic All-Southeastern Conference honors to his growing list of extraordinary accomplishments.

At the conclusion of his senior season, Alan Pizzitola reached the pinnacle of his fantastic walk-on career by earning All-SEC honors at strong safety while repeating as Academic All-SEC. After walking off stage with a diploma for the bachelor's degree he earned in four years, Alan went right to work at establishing himself in a business career.

FROM THE FIELD TO THE OFFICE

Retaining the hard-work ethic of the hungry walk-on he once was, Alan scheduled 22 job interviews, which ultimately led to three safe offers he liked and one atypical offer that gave him second thoughts. Alan received no rejections during this career courtship; it was he who passed on the other 18 companies. The offer that stood out was the most lucrative but least interesting to Alan: selling low-cost office supplies (rubber bands, paper clips, pencils and pens) throughout the state of Alabama. He accepted that nonglamorous opportunity anyway (Dad said the extra money was too good to pass up.) and worked his way up to the office furniture division. Ten years later, Alan signed over to a local bank every major financial asset he owned as collateral to start his own company—Business Interiors Inc.—which today is the largest office furniture dealership in the state of Alabama.

GREAT TEAMMATES AND TEACHERS

Alan attributes Business Interiors' success to his great team of colleagues and employees, his much-appreciated clients and friends, and the many valuable lessons he learned from Coach Bryant, who told his Crimson Tide teams, "Guys, do you get it? Sure, we're here to play good football. But this isn't just about football. We're here to teach you about being good men—to help you know what to do when you leave this place."

Alan has applied Bear Bryant's football/life lessons for more than 35 years in business: "It's really no different in business. You need a plan that you believe in. You set ambitious goals. You come to work every day on time and prepared. You practice and work harder than others, particularly when you hit the inevitable bumps in the road. And then the results take care of themselves. Coach Bryant didn't emphasize winning.

He always said, 'Winning takes care of itself.' He emphasized doing all the little things it takes to win."

Today, Alan wishes he could tell Coach Bryant how much he and his teammates (now in their 50s) still appreciate the fantastic opportunity they had playing for him, the priceless life lessons they learned, and the support they'll always remember. Paul William "Bear" Bryant died suddenly at the age of 69, just one month after retiring from a 25-year head coaching career at the University of Alabama, where he amassed 6 national championships and 13 conference championships. Upon his retirement in 1982, he held the record for the most wins in collegiate football history.

Another major supporter Alan appreciates is Bill Crawford, the entrepreneur who took him under his wing right out of college, hired him, and taught him the office furniture business. Bill took great care of Alan, brought him to social events, and treated him like a son. In return, Crawford received from Alan the hard work and results he needed to grow his business. Although their paths eventually diverged (they actually became competitors), Alan remains extremely thankful for Crawford's caring mentorship in the early years and his good friendship today.

THERE'S NO PLACE LIKE HOME

Perhaps Alan Pizzitola's greatest supporter, and the person he appreciates as much as anyone for giving him a solid foundation early in life, is his father. To this day, Alan, his brother, and their father eat dinner together every Monday night at the same Italian restaurant. This simple tradition gives Alan and his brother an easy way to thank their father for a lifetime of support.

Alan's mother also played a key leadership role in the early formation of his character and work ethic. His wife, Suzanne, who understands the office furniture business firsthand because she worked in it, stays in his corner through the inevitable ups and downs of successful entrepreneurship. And their daughters, Maggy and Laura, make Alan's family life complete—plus the two of them cheer even louder for the Crimson Tide than he does.

THE OLD GRINDSTONE

Hard work is one of the values that Alan's father and mother instilled in him. In response to the question "What differentiates Business Interiors from other companies that provide similar products and services?" Alan simply replied, "No one outprepares us, and no one outworks us." One recent new hire lasted only 3½ months before calling Alan and saying, "I made a mistake joining this company. Y'all just work too hard for me."

GOOD JUGGLING

In these demanding times with 24-7 global businesses, continuous online access, and the expectation of short and sweet responses at work, home, and play, all work and no balance makes most of us unhappy. Just as he balanced being a student and an athlete in college, Alan Pizzitola the businessperson has balanced his professional and personal lives, staying true to his family values while succeeding as a business owner and salesperson. For example, he was known to excuse himself early from business meetings in order to make the start of athletic events in which his children played.

GIVING BACK

As a business owner and philanthropist, Alan also enjoys helping others succeed. At work, he says he strives to be more of a coach and facilitator, who leads people to self-discovery and long-term growth, than a boss and manager, who just tells others what to do for temporary solutions. Outside of work, he has "given back" as an active member of humanitarian organizations such as the Kiwanis Club and the Leukemia & Lymphoma Society and as a generous donor to other causes.

BODY, MIND AND . . .

Applying the concept of balance to another context, Alan translates the "healthy living" concepts he learned as a student-athlete into a balanced combination of physical and intellectual activities that suit him well today. Success as a student-athlete under Bear Bryant depended a great deal on peak physical conditioning and mental toughness; the Crimson Tide followed a demanding training regimen that included endurance running, wind sprints, weight lifting, and proper nutrition, none of it optional. To succeed as a businessperson, Alan makes sure to eat right and get the rest and health care he needs to sustain a productive and enjoyable pace.

Alan and his Business Interiors colleagues keep their business minds sharp with active participation in seminars and conferences and through consultation with outside experts. This continuous professional development helps them stay current with the latest general management thinking and specific industry trends.

AN EXEMPLAR

The Alan Pizzitola success story is a perfect example of the great heights underdogs can hit when they remain resilient in the face of adversity, develop greater self-confidence, and turn short-term success into a long-term habit. If Paul William "Bear" Bryant could see Alan today, he'd probably agree.

BOB BLEYER
COMMUNITY BUSINESS LEADER

*Notre Dame Fighting Irish
coached by Dan Devine*

*"Your application for
admission to Notre Dame
has been denied"*

IT'S IN THE BLOOD

Bob Bleyer's love of Notre Dame football began during childhood as he sat glued to the TV for Sunday morning highlights of every game. "There was never a question in my mind or a decision to be made about where I'd go to college," he says. "My oldest brother's name is Knute Rockne Bleyer, and my second oldest brother's name is Frank Leahy Bleyer."

In case you're not up on Fighting Irish football history, legendary coaches Knute Rockne and Frank Leahy combined for 192 victories, a winning percentage of 83, and seven consensus national championships between 1918 and 1953. They set the standard for Notre Dame's six Hall of Fame head coaches. For most college football zealots, Rockne symbolizes the institution of college football coaching (along with such legends as Paul "Bear" Bryant of Alabama, and Bobby Bowden of Florida State).

"My father and my uncle went to Notre Dame," Bob continues. "Now in their late 70s, they still live and die every football Saturday depending on the outcome of the ND game. Their devotion to the university is incredible. Between my dad, my uncle, their children, and their grandchildren, 12 members of our family have gone there. So you see, I was born to go to Notre Dame."

Bob's father had been a student manager for ND coaching great Frank Leahy before becoming head coach of the Carbondale High Terriers in southern Illinois. It was with the Terriers that Bob starred at fullback in the mid '70s, playing on the gridiron that had been named Bleyer Field after his father's retirement in the late '60s. Despite earning All State honors for his senior season, Bob lacked the complete package of dominant size, speed, and strength required to be recruited by major college programs. But with desire and a work ethic that rivaled those of any scholarship player, Bob was quietly confident he could succeed as a walk-on with the Fighting Irish.

Then the unthinkable happened: "When I applied to Notre Dame in 1976, *I didn't get accepted.*"

FROM MIDWEST TO EAST AND BACK

In his high school years in Carbondale (with a 2010 population of 25,902), Bob—like many smart students who earn high grades—didn't excel on standardized college entrance exams. So after getting a rejection letter from Notre Dame, he switched to Plan B: a year of boarding school at Northfield Mount Hermon (NMH) in Massachusetts. An 18-year-old kid from a small Midwestern town, Bob felt a bit out of place at one of New England's oldest and most prestigious college preparatory schools. But he was on a mission. He had set ambitious goals to excel on the football field and in the classroom, enough to earn admission to Notre Dame after completing a special "postgraduate" year of studies.

Bob's accelerated enculturation at NMH, with its student body of future Ivy Leaguers and a faculty stocked with Ivy alumni, included more accolades on the football field along with a newly discovered talent. He summed it up sarcastically: "It's really amazing how much your SAT scores can jump after you take a special prep course before the test." With his scores 25 percent higher, Bob got recruited to play football for the Cornell Big Red, the Dartmouth Big Green, and the Princeton Tigers. NMH's headmaster encouraged him to take advantage of an opportunity to join the ranks of the Ivy League, with its instant prestige, worldwide alumni network, and lifetime of open doors.

But Bob was a Bleyer, and Bleyers went to Notre Dame. So he reapplied for admission and a chance to try out for the Fighting Irish, and this time the answer came back—yes! Bob believed his dream was about to come true as he headed west to South Bend, Indiana.

SCOUT'S HONOR

Bob's college football career began on the "scout team"—also known as the "practice squad"—as a freshman in 1977. Scout team players have the unenviable task of impersonating the next opponent during practice all week so the "real" players—first, second, and third stringers—get a good preview of what they'll likely see in Saturday's game. Being a walk-on member of the scout team comes with about as much glory and insider status as being picked last for dodge ball in junior high gym class, struggling to get a word in as the youngest member of big family during a heated dinner discussion, or walking in late on the first day of high school homeroom as the new transfer from across town.

Playing scout team is actually a critically important role on any great football team, but it takes a special kind of toughness to stick it out and succeed. Most scout players—be they walk-ons or scholarship winners—last a year or two before burning out, getting seriously injured, or both. Bob believed he would eventually be good enough to play for the Irish varsity squad on Saturdays, with outstanding performance on the scout team as his ticket to the real action.

"At first, playing scout team was actually quite scary, to tell you the truth," Bob recalled. A harsh dose of reality greeted him and the other freshmen during their first week of practice in the summer heat and humidity. They all, scholarship and walk-on players alike, were relegated to dressing and showering in a second-rate, freshmen-only locker room. Ahead of Bob on the depth chart were superstar running backs Vegas Ferguson and Jerome Heavens, followed by a long list of backups. The first time Bob's coach called his number to run a live play for the scout team offense, the untouched walk-on anxiously looked up and saw on the other side of the line of scrimmage current and future All Americans Luther Bradley, Ross Browner, Willie Fry, and Bob Golic peering at him like sharks sizing up a lost seal. "What in the world am I doing here?" he asked himself. It was sobering for 19-year-old Bob to realize that after being among the best high school players in Illinois and New England, at Notre Dame he would have to beat out some of the best college players in the nation.

That ended up being a highly successful season for Notre Dame. In the Cotton Bowl, the Fighting Irish beat the Texas Longhorns and Heisman Trophy–winning running back Earl Campbell. Notre Dame also took home its tenth national championship, with a quarterback by the name of Joe Montana.

GETTING SERIOUS

To survive and eventually succeed in that kind of championship environment, Bob knew he had to intensify his work habits. He had never shied away from hard work before, but now he had to raise his weight lifting, endurance running, nutrition, and overall physical and mental toughness to their highest levels. Bob planned to patiently wait for the older guys to graduate, outwork the scholarship players who were his age or younger, and then get his chance to get in the game. He set a goal to play fullback in Notre Dame Stadium on Saturdays—not for the scout team on the practice field Monday through Friday.

Bob thought he had made his mark at the end of his sophomore year with a convincing performance in the Blue-Gold scrimmage. Spring practice culminated in this annual rite of passage and let everyone know who would likely start, or at least get significant playing time, the following fall. At fullback that day, Bob punished the opposition while opening wide running lanes for his tailback, who rushed for over 100 yards against the first-team defense. Running backs coach Jim Gruden (2003 Super Bowl champion coach Jon Gruden's father) let Bob know right away that he played a great game. The starting fullback, who blew out his knee in the scrimmage, admitted, "I don't think I'll be able to play this fall." So Bob thought to himself, "This is my chance." And he made up his mind right then and there to train in the off-season like never before so that he would report to summer camp in the best shape of his life.

When Bob Bleyer returned to South Bend for his junior season, the duly impressed athletic trainers welcomed him back in amazement: "What in the [h***] have you done to your body?" But it wasn't just good looks. Bob's bench press now approached 400 pounds and his squats topped 550. In the 40-yard dash he held his own against the other fullbacks, even keeping up with some of the backup tailbacks. Bob's new sense of accomplishment, growing confidence, and high expectations felt good. He felt even better the next day when Coach Gruden told him to lead his teammates through their warm-up exercises.

GUT PUNCH

Then, on the third morning, the depth chart went up on the locker room wall, and Bob's dream crashed down. After three grueling summers of training harder than he'd ever trained, after two seasons of running plays at 100 percent effort for the merciless scout team, after cheering his lungs out from the stands (not the sidelines) at every game, after an outstanding performance during the Blue-Gold spring scrimmage, and after leading his teammates through warm-ups on the second day of camp, "Bleyer" appeared as fifth string—with three freshmen scholarship fullbacks ahead of him. They had already topped him in only their first week of their first year on the team. "And that was the end of it," Bob remembered, seeming almost as devastated now (32 years later) as he says he felt then. It was a big surprise for many who were there, and a bigger disappointment for Bob. Even Coach Gruden said to him, "Bob I'm going to do everything I can to at least get you a spot on special teams because you deserve it."

"I wasn't going to quit, no matter what," a still-resilient Bob recalled. "I still believed I could play on special teams at some point during my junior season." But Bob never saw game action on special teams or as a backup fullback that year. It ended up being the third long season in a row devoted to the scout team, where the most he could do was help his teammates prepare to succeed on Saturdays.

DREAMS DO COME TRUE

After that personally disappointing season, Bob began to flirt with the possibility of hanging up his cleats for good. With three freshmen already ahead of him, and more blue-chip recruits coming the next year, he naturally thought, "I'm never going to play at

Notre Dame. Maybe I should just quit." But eventually he realized, "I don't want to live with the 'quitter' label for the rest of my life." So not only did he not quit, he recommitted to thinking, talking, and acting as though he still had a chance to get in the game. "I decided to keep practicing and working out as hard as anybody on the team because you just never know what can happen. I kept dreaming. If my chance ever came, I wanted to be ready. I never wanted to look back and wish I had worked harder or prepared better. I didn't want to have any regrets."

Bob's senior season proved to be immeasurably better than the preceding three. He dressed for half the home games and won the Player of the Week Award for his outstanding scout team performance before the Georgia Tech game. It was hard to tell who was happiest about the award—Bob, his teammates, or the coaches. Then on November 22, 1980, against the Air Force Falcons, in front of a capacity crowd at Notre Dame Stadium, Bob Bleyer's lifelong dream finally came true. In that final home game of the year, at the end of the fourth quarter, on the last series of downs, Coach Dan Devine gave him the green light: "Bleyer, get in there!" As Bob fastened his chin strap and sprinted to the huddle, friends in the Fighting Irish student section rose to their feet, cheering in unison "Rah-key, Rah-key, Rah-key!" (During his freshman

year, Bob's teammates and classmates had affection-
ately nicknamed him "Rocky" after Fighting Irish and
Pittsburgh Steelers great Rocky Bleier).

Bob didn't do anything spectacular during his three
plays on the gridiron that afternoon, but he did make
his teammates, coaches, fans, and himself beam with
pride; Notre Dame won the game 24-10. Taking his
dream one cloud higher to end the season, Bob finally
made the travel team—for the Sugar Bowl against
future Heisman Trophy winner Herschel Walker and
the Georgia Bulldogs—on January 1, 1981. Georgia
won that game 17-10, finishing the year a perfect 11-0
and winning the national championship.

By the time Bob and his senior teammates ended
the season, their original freshmen class of about 30
scholarship and three walk-on players had dwindled
down to nine scholarship players and one walk-on,
Bob Bleyer. For his unwavering dedication, role-model
work ethic, and constant resilience, Bob earned a varsity letter to go along with the national championship
ring from his freshman year. Moments after the Sugar
Bowl ended, Bob talked with his teammates in the
locker room about the finality of their season and his
Notre Dame career. "As I sat in front of my locker for
the last time and thought about everything I had been
through at Notre Dame, I couldn't believe it was really

over. My eyes welled up, and I didn't want to take off my uniform."

ROLE MODEL ON AND OFF THE FIELD

At the year-end awards banquet, Head Coach Dan Devine introduced each member of the senior class and said something complimentary about his playing career at Notre Dame. When Bob Bleyer's turn came, Devine described him as a four-year walk-on, a role model who gave everything he had to help his teammates succeed on Saturdays. "I couldn't have asked for anything more from a player," he said. When the crowd broke into a standing ovation, "It felt better than if I had scored 10 touchdowns that season," the still-humble Bob said with a smile. Although Bob did not bask in the traditional glory of Notre Dame football stardom, he had earned something that many consider more impressive and desirable: the respect and admiration of his teammates, coaches, classmates, and fans. "When it was all said and done, I was really happy I did it. Today, I have absolutely no regrets," he says.

Bob Bleyer became a role model for hard work, dedication, and discipline, which is why so many teammates—scholarship and nonscholarship—asked if they could train with him in the off-season. As a Fighting Irish football player, Bob worked harder than he ever had in his life, and this work ethic would later serve him well as a business leader. Another walk-on benefit that served Bob well, after he put away his uniform for good, was his Notre Dame education, with its strong academics, lifelong friendships, and huge network of passionate alumni and fans. (In fact, *The Wall Street Journal* has cited Notre Dame as one of the "New Ivies" in American higher education along with, among others, Duke and Northwestern.)

Perhaps more impressive than his football accomplishments is the fact that Bob graduated with honors as an accounting and finance major, posting a 3.7 grade point average in the College of Business. This academic achievement did not come easily. Bob says he probably worked even harder in the classroom and the library than he did in the weight room and on the football field.

A KEY TAKEAWAY

"It all comes down to this," Bob says. "If playing football for Notre Dame taught me one thing, it's that you can compete with anybody, in anything you put your mind to, if you work hard enough. I really believe that, and I proved it to myself by keeping up with the high school valedictorians from across the country who filled the hallways of Notre Dame. It was a standard routine for me to go from early morning classes, to afternoon football practice or weight training, to dinner, to the library until midnight, and then to bed— five days a week. On weekends, though, I made time for lots of fun with my teammates and my friends from Dillon Hall. We really had a great time."

SUPPORTING CAST

Bob knows he benefited from the support of key individuals during his uphill football career at Notre Dame—from being an unknown freshman walk-on to earning a varsity letter as a senior. Scholarship teammates and peers—including tight end Marty Detmer, strong safety Bill Doran, quarterback Tim Koegel, and offensive tackle Steve LaHam—accepted and respected Bob as if he were a scholarship player.

At the low point of Bob's sophomore season, his dad, the former Coach Bleyer, could tell Bob was down after not getting much playing time during a junior varsity game (essentially a weekday scrimmage between opposing scout team players whose varsity teams would square off that Saturday). Afterward, Father put his arm around Son and said, "When your coach told you to get in the game, I noticed that six other players came up to you and said, 'Go get 'em, Rock.' You know, that's a great thing, because it shows how much your teammates respect you. Most players never earn that, so remember it and be proud."

MORE HARD WORK

As committed as Bob is to the University of Notre Dame, he may be even more loyal to the community of Carbondale, where he still lives and works. A former certified public accountant, Bob leads the Bank of Carbondale as its president and CEO. He took the helm of this community business after years of applying the lessons he learned as a walk-on. "In order to be successful in business, I knew I simply had to outwork everybody like I did on the football field and in the classroom," he remembers matter-of-factly. "As a CPA during tax season, sometimes I had to work past midnight and then be back on the job at 7 a.m. When I started working at the bank, 12-hour days, six days a week, became the norm. Adding to that already heavy load, I went to night school for an MBA." Bob essentially carried his extraordinary work ethic out of the locker room and into the office. He does the same with his ambitious goals. Now, every year the Bank of Carbondale breaks earnings records, President Bleyer simply says to his executive team, "Great, let's do it again."

FAILURE WAS NOT AN OPTION

But things at the bank weren't always so good. Bob's well-intentioned father, a part owner, bought out all of his partners in 1981—not a very good year for community banks. 1982, '83, and '84 weren't much better. The elder Bleyer became so overleveraged that bankruptcy stared him in the face. If the Bank of Carbondale had failed, much of the small-business community of Carbondale—which depended on the bank's loans to operate successfully—might not have been far behind. When federal regulators got wind of the situation, they issued an edict: fix the bank in six months, or we'll shut you down. That's when 25-year-old Bob Bleyer had to quit working at his CPA firm to join the bank as its new president. Bob's charge was simple: Save the bank, or his father loses everything he worked for over a lifetime. Save the bank, or the Bleyer family loses its net worth. Save the bank, or one of the pillars of this proud town—the Bank of Carbondale, chartered in 1919—comes crumbling down.

Most 25-year-olds don't carry such weight on their shoulders. But thanks to his walk-on experience, Bob Bleyer was not like most 25-year-olds. In his case, "failure was not an option." So he spent about four hours a night in the library, week after week, teaching himself about the banking industry. He developed a turnaround plan for the Bank of Carbondale and then sold the plan to the federal regulators. At six-month intervals, Bob reported progress to the regulators until they finally took him, and the Bank of Carbondale, out of their fishbowl of scrutiny after two years. "If I hadn't accomplished what I did at Notre Dame, I never would have had the motivation, the stamina, or the confidence to pull off the bank turnaround," he says.

ALSO FOCUSED ON FAMILY

At that point in his life Bob wasn't married with children, so he was able to work ungodly hours without sacrificing family time. When he married Lori—also a CPA at his former firm and no stranger to long hours—and they later had three children, Bob did his best to fully engage in fatherhood from dinnertime until bedtime. Then he often went back to work at the bank from 9 p.m. until midnight. A wise uncle had cautioned him years earlier: "You'll never find a man on his deathbed who says, 'I wish I would have worked more and spent less time with my family.'" So Bob spent as much time as he could with his wife and children, Patrick, Nic, and Emily. He gladly did everything from coach the kids' little league teams to tuck them in at night, by "giving up most other things and not sleeping much," he recalls with an honest smile before adding, "In the end, everything turned out great."

STILL IN GREAT SHAPE

Bob still stays healthy with a daily exercise regimen of 30 minutes of cardiovascular training in the morning before work and 30 minutes of weight lifting during lunch. He also tries to maintain a nutritious diet (but admits to slipping now and then, like the rest of us). Bob believes his healthy lifestyle helps him perform well not only in his professional and personal lives but also as a volunteer assistant wrestling coach at Carbondale High. Coach Bob Bleyer, at the young and strong age of 52, has been known to give some of the Terrier teenage grapplers all they can handle on the practice mat.

GREAT TEAM AT WORK

President and CEO Bleyer appreciates the ongoing support he's received from his team of employees at the Bank of Carbondale. In what has essentially become a commoditized business, they sustain their success with a unique brand of customer service. And how, precisely, do they define success? Well, one telling indicator is asset growth (assets such as loans, cash, and investments). When Bob took over the failing bank in 1984, assets amounted to a paltry $18 million. By 2009 they had grown to a robust $190 million. That's more than a tenfold increase (or 955 percent)! Federal bank regulators paid Bob and his executive team a routine visit in 2009 and assured them that their bank had outperformed over 50 percent of the other banks in the state of Illinois during that economically depressed year.

CUSTOMER SERVICE BREEDS LOYALTY

"Our success is not just because of me or what I do," Bob says. "If our team was not liked by our customers, and if we didn't deliver good service, we'd be out of business. I tell my team that as much as I can. It's very important to let them know that they, and what they do, are vital."

Members of their loyal customer base, which falls within a radius of only 20 miles, have assured Bob that when other banks call, the answer is simple: "I will never leave the Bank of Carbondale." That's the essence of community banking—earned customer loyalty and the referrals that come from it. As president, Bob sees any customer who would like to talk directly with him. "The one thing I appreciate more than anything is the loyalty of our customers. We need them to survive, but they don't need us; they can go to any bank." As a respected community business leader, Bob is often asked, "What's the best thing about a career in banking?" The No. 1 answer he gives is, "In the community banking business, when your customers succeed, there's just no better feeling."

FROM PLAYER TO COACH

Same goes for his personal life. Bob loves helping his children, and the other children and young adults of Carbondale, succeed in athletics. He has coached soccer, baseball, and wrestling—and even started the Carbondale little league football program from scratch. As a father, Bob encouraged his own children to participate in athletics so they could benefit from the priceless lessons of the locker room, weight room, practice field, and stadium. True athletes know that what goes on in these venues can occasionally have more impact than the best parents or teachers. Bob says simply, "If it wasn't for what I learned in athletics, I would not be where I am today."

PREPARING THE NEXT GENERATION

It appears that the next generation of apples hasn't fallen far from the Bleyer family tree. Bob's and Lori's two sons and daughter have excelled in the classroom and on the field, as indicated by high GPAs and ACT scores along with MVP awards and captain roles. These outstanding achievements can be attributed, in part, to two of Bob's favorite foundational rules: "No. 1 is if you do something, do the best you can. Don't waste your time or anyone else's if you're not going to give your best effort. No. 2 is if you start something, finish it. Don't just quit in the beginning or middle if it's challenging or you don't like it."

THE UNDERDOG IN ALL OF US

The Bob Bleyer success story isn't really one of glory, popularity, or stardom. It's more about confronting challenges and overcoming obstacles with inner strength, honest hard work, remarkable perseverance, and humility. By any measure, Bob was a talented football player with an above-average intellect, but what made him an extraordinarily successful walk-on, community business leader, and family man is *what he did with what he was given*. Doesn't this principle ring true for all of us?

THEIR WINNING STRATEGIES

VALUABLE LESSONS LEARNED FROM WALK-ONS

Now it's time to summarize the valuable lessons we can learn from the inspirational stories of our former walk-ons. We'll also see what some of the world's human performance experts say about how these great ideas can help us *do* better and *feel* better at work and home.

Gordon Adams, Bob Bleyer, and Alan Pizzitola graduated from storied universities in the 1970s and '80s with academic honors, national championship rings, practical skills, and a collection of winning strategies that helped them persevere and succeed in business and life in their 20s, 30s, 40s, and 50s. Seven strategies identified from their experiences can help all of us work through the inevitable ups and downs of business ambition while leaving us with a healthy perspective on what's ultimately important in life.

Businesspeople, sports fans, current and former athletes—and all those who want more out of their professional and personal lives—can become more successful and fulfilled by applying this wisdom.

As you read about the *seven winning strategies*, please relate them to your own life and think about how you can put them to good use.

1. LEVERAGE YOUR STRENGTHS

". . . only when you operate from strengths can you achieve true excellence."

Peter Drucker

THE WALK-ONS LEVERAGED THEIR STRENGTHS

The walk-ons understood, accepted, and leveraged their strengths by 1) trying out for the positions they played best and 2) putting their natural abilities to good use on and off the field. They did not force themselves into bad-fit situations to please others or fulfill unrealistic self-ideals.

REVIEW: AN EXAMPLE FROM COLLEGE

Alan Pizzitola's strengths in the classroom helped him move from the outer circle to the inner circle among his teammates. As an informal tutor, he received regular invitations from the scholarship players to study with them in the athletes' dorm. The more he helped them with their schoolwork, the more they accepted him in the locker room and on the field.

REVIEW: AN EXAMPLE FROM BUSINESS

Making the transition from quarterback on the field to quarterback in the office has been "a perfect fit," Gordon Adams says. For most of his career, Adams's success has depended on his natural ability to assemble and unite diverse talented teams to solve relatively sophisticated business problems.

EXPERT ADVICE ABOUT LEVERAGING YOUR STRENGTHS

After graduating from Cambridge University with a master's degree in social and political science, Marcus Buckingham spent nearly two decades at the Gallup Organization, where he and his colleagues conducted research on some of the world's best performers and workplaces. In 2007, Buckingham wrote *Go Put Your Strengths to Work: 6 Powerful Steps to Achieve Outstanding Performance*, a practical guide for people who want to understand and apply their strengths for maximum success. Buckingham suggests that people thrive only by building on strengths, not by simply correcting weaknesses. He also tells us that these strengths can be found in the specific activities people consistently do extremely well *and* find fulfilling.

If you don't yet know your strengths, think about the specific activities you consistently do extremely well *and* find fulfilling at work, home, and school—including hobbies and volunteer activities—and see what patterns you discover. Ask people who are familiar with what you do to offer their candid opinions and ideas. An honest self-assessment combined with the perceptions of others you trust will give you good insight.

For those of us who could use some help, there's Donald O. Clifton, who was honored with an American Psychological Association Presidential Commendation as "the father of strengths-based psychology" for his lifelong work on helping people to discover and leverage their strengths. Dr. Clifton and his team created an insightful assessment tool—originally called the "StrengthsFinder"—based on 40 years of Gallup research.

In 2007, Gallup Consulting Global Practice leader Tom Rath authored *The Wall Street Journal* bestseller *StrengthsFinder 2.0*. This version of the assessment includes a personalized report of one's top five strengths, an action-planning guide, and access to a web-based community.

2. SET STRETCH GOALS

". . . unless you set the bar high enough, you'll never find out what [you] can do."

Jack Welch

THE WALK-ONS SET STRETCH GOALS

The walk-ons stretched themselves to accomplish challenging, rewarding goals. They didn't just take the safe or easy road.

REVIEW: AN EXAMPLE FROM COLLEGE

After getting his rejection letter from Notre Dame's admissions office, Bob Bleyer switched to Plan B: a year of boarding school at Northfield Mount Hermon. Bleyer was on a mission. He had set ambitious goals to excel on the football field and in the classroom, enough to earn admission to Notre Dame after completing this special "postgraduate" year of studies. When he reapplied for admission to Notre Dame and a chance to try out for the Fighting Irish, the answer came back—yes!

REVIEW: AN EXAMPLE FROM BUSINESS

Ten years after graduating from the University of Alabama, Alan Pizzitola decided to start his own company. He signed over to a local bank every major financial asset he owned as collateral in order to open Business Interiors Inc. Today, it's the largest office furniture dealership in Alabama.

EXPERT ADVICE ABOUT SETTING STRETCH GOALS

Marshall Goldsmith—recognized as a global authority for helping people achieve positive, lasting behavior change—was named one of the world's most influential business thinkers by *The (London) Times* and *Forbes*, one of the great leaders to influence the field of management by the American Management Association, and one of the top executive educators by *The Wall Street Journal*. In his 2009 bestseller *MOJO: How to Get It, How to Keep It, How to Get It Back If You Lose It*, Dr. Goldsmith explains that many people give up on goal achievement when they're faced with inevitable obstacles such as time, effort, other priorities, temptation to stop after initial progress, unsatisfactory rewards, and the need for maintenance. He encourages goal setters to be ready for these normal challenges, stay resilient when they appear, and achieve!

In my own workplace learning and performance improvement work at Northwestern University, I coach individuals, groups, and organizations to set "SMART" goals and review them regularly:

S = Specific: clear and easy to understand

M = Measureable: recognizable, with a number or other success indicator

A = Achievable: realistic

R = Relevant: important, with a link to your values or mission

T = Time-bound: moved forward, with a due date

3. WORK HARD

". . . the best investment [you] can possibly make is . . . just plain, hard work."

Charles Schwab

THE WALK-ONS WORKED HARD

The walk-ons worked hard, often harder than others, to overcome adversity. They did not stop short or give up altogether when the going got tough.

REVIEW: AN EXAMPLE FROM COLLEGE

Bob Bleyer set an example in the classroom as well as on the field, graduating with a 3.7 grade point average. "If playing football for Notre Dame taught me one thing, it's that you can compete with anybody, in anything you put your mind to, if you work hard enough. I really believe that, and I proved it to myself by keeping up with the high school valedictorians from across the country who filled the hallways of Notre Dame. It was a standard routine for me to go from early morning classes, to afternoon football practice or weight training, to dinner, to the library until midnight, and then to bed—five days a week."

REVIEW: AN EXAMPLE FROM BUSINESS

Gordon Adams knows that his father was right about the value of hard work. "My dad always said, 'Whatever you do, do your best, do it right, do it to the fullest, and don't quit.' I followed his advice [as a walk-on], and I still apply it today." For walk-ons and businesspeople alike, Adams says, sustained success depends a great deal on habitual hard work, continuous learning, and perseverance. Walk-ons can't afford to let up when they're surrounded by eager scholarship players loaded with talent, just as businesspeople can't rest on their laurels in a competitive and dynamic marketplace. "If you work hard, do the right things, and have confidence, you'll eventually get your opportunity," Adams asserts. "And when it comes, you better be prepared to take advantage of it. You have to simultaneously be patient and maintain an inner drive to be the best you can be."

EXPERT ADVICE ABOUT WORKING HARD

Mihaly Csikszentmihalyi is Distinguished Professor of Psychology and Management and founder of the Quality of Life Research Center at the Claremont Graduate University. While at the University of Chicago as professor and former chair of the psychology department in 1990, he published *Flow: The Psychology of Optimal Experience*. Dr. Csikszentmihalyi's influential work applied modern psychology to an ancient question: What makes people truly happy? He and his colleagues studied thousands of individuals around the world from different walks of life. They concluded that our most gratifying moments occur when we push ourselves through difficultly to accomplish worthwhile things. The positive outcomes eventually justify the challenging (and sometimes unpleasant) processes.

4. STAY BALANCED

"The best and safest thing is to keep a balance in your life . . . If you can do that . . . you are really a wise [person]."

Euripides

THE WALK-ONS STAYED BALANCED

The walk-ons, as true student-athletes, had to stay balanced by succeeding in the classroom and on the football field. If they had focused too much on one or the other, they would have come up short overall.

REVIEW: AN EXAMPLE FROM COLLEGE

Gordon Adams says that he learned the "work-hard-play-hard" rule as a Trojan. "I could have fun when it was time to have fun, but I had to really work hard when it was time to work." So how well did Adams balance the sometimes competing demands of being a student and an athlete? While building a remarkable career on the football field, he won the team award for highest cumulative grade point average among letter-men in both his junior and senior years—and ended up graduating with a 3.7 GPA as a business major.

REVIEW: AN EXAMPLE FROM BUSINESS

As a young family man, Bob Bleyer spent as much time as possible with his wife and children, doing everything from coaching the kids' little league teams to tucking them in at night. He tried to live by the words of his wise uncle: "You'll never find a man on his deathbed who says 'I wish I would have worked more and spent less time with my family.'"

EXPERT ADVICE ABOUT STAYING BALANCED

James O'Toole is the Daniels Distinguished Professor of Business Ethics at the University of Denver's Daniels College of Business. O'Toole received his doctorate in social anthropology from Oxford University, where he was a Rhodes Scholar. In 2005—while a research professor in the Center for Effective Organizations at the University of Southern California and the Mortimer J. Adler Senior Fellow of the Aspen

Institute—he published *Creating the Good Life: Applying Aristotle's Wisdom to Find Meaning and Happiness*. This insightful writing offers Dr. O'Toole's take on how Aristotle's timeless teachings from the fourth century B.C. help people live well today. O'Toole and Aristotle suggest that true success and fulfillment depend not only on the extent to which we lead balanced lives of work, family and leisure but also on whether we help others. Perhaps the old adage "All work and no play makes Jack a dull boy" could use an additional phrase: "And no service to others will eventually make Jack feel empty."

Real balance requires clear values and occasionally difficult choices about tradeoffs. For example, a businessperson who truly values family before work might leave the office at 5 p.m. to make his daughter's school play, even if that means missing a dinner meeting with a key client. In this case, her lifetime memory ("My dad was there for opening night.") would be more valuable than his short-term financial gain ("The dinner deal could have paid me a $5,000 bonus that quarter."). When faced with this understandably difficult decision, the dad may say to himself, "There will always be other prospective clients to see, different deals to close, and bigger paychecks to earn over the course of a career. But there may be only one school play and only one chance to experience it with my daughter, who will be fully grown and out of the house before I know it."

5. BE HEALTHY

"A wise [person] should consider that health is the greatest of human blessings . . ."

Hippocrates

THE WALK-ONS WERE HEALTHY

The walk-ons had to stay healthy by eating right, exercising and training regularly, and getting enough rest. The physical (and emotional) demands placed on them were too great to have done otherwise.

REVIEW: AN EXAMPLE FROM COLLEGE

Alan Pizzitola followed a daily regimen of endurance running, wind sprints, and weight lifting to get ready for his freshman tryout with the University of Alabama. He had a difficult goal to achieve: arrive at summer practice in Tuscaloosa in top condition, able to pass every test the Crimson Tide coaches threw at him. Then success as a student-athlete under Bear Bryant depended a great deal on peak physical conditioning and mental toughness.

REVIEW: AN EXAMPLE FROM BUSINESS

Bob Bleyer still stays healthy with a daily exercise regimen that features cardiovascular training in the morning before work and weight lifting during lunch. He also tries to maintain a nutritious diet. Bob believes his healthy lifestyle helps him perform well not only in his professional and personal lives but also as a volunteer assistant wrestling coach at Carbondale High. Coach Bob Bleyer, at age 52, has been known to give some of the teenage grapplers all they can handle on the practice mat.

EXPERT ADVICE ABOUT BEING HEALTHY

While most of us know that getting regular exercise and eating a balanced diet can improve vitality and help prevent disease, not enough of us seem to *actually do* these things consistently. You may have heard the joke that "Americans will do anything to get healthy except exercise more and eat less." Why is this so often the case? Paul M. Insel and Walton T. Roth—faculty members at Stanford University—published their 12th edition of *Connect Core Concepts in Health* in 2011. For over 30 years, this personal-health text has provided scientifically based answers and guidelines. Drs. Insel and Roth say it may seem too hard to change our unhealthy behavior at first. But by sticking with it and making progress, we gain confidence and build momentum. Then the benefits of wellness kick in as we feel better, have more energy, and eventually experience a higher quality of life.

After embracing the idea that we need to exercise regularly and eat well to help sustain true success and fulfillment in our lives, we need to motivate ourselves to take action. This self-motivation can come from a strong enough belief that the benefits of living healthier (a longer, happier, and more productive existence) outweigh the costs (it takes time and effort). Once we're committed, then a simple written plan—with realistic goals and actions—can give us the clarity and confidence we need to stay on track. For example:

*Goal (**what** I want to accomplish):*

- *I will lose 5 pounds of fat by August 1—and keep it off!*

*Actions (**how** I will accomplish the goal):*

- *I will "speed walk" 2 miles, or "ride fast" on my exercise bike 6 miles if the weather is bad, 5 days a week.*

- *I will eat no more than 1 small dessert item a day.*

Many people improve the likelihood of successfully implementing their plans by partnering with friends who 1) have similar goals and actions and 2) encourage them to keep going when inevitable obstacles tempt them to pull back or quit.

6. APPRECIATE YOUR SUPPORTERS

". . . it's easy for [people] to get blinded by their own self-importance and lose a sense of . . . teamwork."

Phil Jackson

THE WALK-ONS APPRECIATED THEIR SUPPORTERS

The walk-ons appreciated their supporters because they knew they could not have succeeded without help from family members, coaches, teammates, friends, and others who cared.

REVIEW: AN EXAMPLE FROM COLLEGE

Alan Pizzitola's all-star support team of family, friends, coaches, and teammates provided the kind of guidance and help in college that he still appreciates today. For example, in his sophomore season, Pizzitola happily (and fortunately) played second-string strong safety behind David McMakin, a senior who mentored him well. Like a good coach, McMakin taught Pizzitola about the often underappreciated strategic aspects of football: studying film of Alabama's opponents, learning their tendencies, reading formations, and anticipating plays.

REVIEW: AN EXAMPLE FROM BUSINESS

Gordon Adams is still grateful to his early supporters, particularly his parents, who instilled motivation, energy, and passion to succeed through the example they set, the guidance they provided, and the excellence they expected. Adams recalls Coach Hackett teaching him one of the major responsibilities of leadership: giving credit to those not in the spotlight, those whose vital contributions usually go unrecognized. Adams does this today by getting to know his business teammates well, letting them know why their contributions are vital, and showing them sincere appreciation.

EXPERT ADVICE ABOUT APPRECIATING YOUR SUPPORTERS

No person achieves true success alone, but too often we forget to 1) treat our supporters well, and 2) let them know how much we appreciate them. Danny Meyer—CEO of Union Square Hospitality Group—is the founder and co-owner of a diverse group of New York City restaurants, which have earned an unprecedented 21 James Beard Awards and perennially rank among New York's favorites in the Zagat survey. In 2006, Meyer shared his unconventional wisdom about business success in *The New York Times* bestseller *Setting the Table: The Transforming Power of Hospitality in Business*. Meyer and his leadership team have built their business model on a foundation of hospitality and appreciation that puts employees first, followed by guests, the community, suppliers, and investors. This "enlightened hospitality" permeates their company culture and guides practically every decision. If our ongoing success depends a great deal on how we make people feel, as Meyer suggests, then we should make sure our supporters feel sincerely appreciated for who they are and what they contribute.

7. HELP OTHERS SUCCEED

"What I know for sure is that what you give comes back to you."

Oprah Winfrey

THE WALK-ONS HELPED OTHERS SUCCEED

The walk-ons first helped their scholarship teammates (and their coaches) succeed in practice and games. That "pay-your-dues-first" investment earned them high returns in the long run.

REVIEW: AN EXAMPLE FROM COLLEGE

Bob Bleyer never saw game action on special teams or as a backup fullback his junior year. It ended up being his third long season in a row on the scout team, where the most he could do was help his teammates prepare to succeed on Saturdays. Then at the awards banquet after Bleyer's final season, head coach Dan Devine introduced each member of the senior class and said something complimentary about his playing career at Notre Dame. When Bleyer's turn came, Devine described him as a four-year walk-on, a role model who gave everything he had to help his teammates succeed on Saturdays. Although Bleyer did not bask in the traditional glory of Notre Dame football stardom, he had earned something that many consider more impressive and desirable: the respect and admiration of his teammates, coaches, classmates, and fans.

REVIEW: AN EXAMPLE FROM BUSINESS

As a business owner and philanthropist, Alan Pizzitola enjoys helping others succeed. At work, he strives to be more of a coach and facilitator who leads people to self-discovery and long-term growth than a boss and manager who just tells others what to do for temporary solutions. Outside of work, he has given back as an active member of humanitarian organizations and as a generous donor to other good causes.

EXPERT ADVICE ABOUT HELPING OTHERS SUCCEED

Stephen R. Covey—recognized worldwide as one of the most influential self-improvement authorities in history—has sold over 20 million books in 38 languages, including his classic *The 7 Habits of Highly Effective People*. Dr. Covey's 2004 work, *The 8th Habit: From Effectiveness to Greatness*, suggests that true fulfillment involves ". . . finding our voice and inspiring others to find theirs." What does this mean? When we do work that leverages our strengths, fuels our passion, and *meets the most significant needs of others*, we succeed by "living our voice." Then we need to inspire others to find and live *their* voices. In other words, part of our movement from effectiveness to greatness depends on the extent to which we help others succeed in this holistic manner. So our true success is not really about, "What's in it for me?" It's more about, "How can I help you?"

YOUR GAME PLAN

Now that you've finished reading *The Wisdom of Walk-Ons*, it's important that you develop a good game plan for what you'll do next—and then implement the plan. The fastest, easiest, and most effective way to do this is to think, talk, and write about what the *seven winning strategies* mean to you. Then regularly revisit what you've written, update it as you wish, and keep moving forward. For convenience, please feel free to copy the format below into your own word processing or spreadsheet software or other tool.

STEP 1: SUMMARIZING WHAT YOU LEARNED

Please summarize below, in your own words, the two most helpful ideas you took away from each of the *seven winning strategies*. To help you get started, here's an example for **leverage your strengths:**

• *A great way to succeed in my career is to identify my greatest strengths, appreciate them, and apply them in current and future jobs.*

1. Leverage your strengths:

• _____

• _____

2. Set stretch goals:

• _____

• _____

3. Work hard:

• _____

• _____

4. Stay balanced:

- _____

- _____

5. Be healthy:

- _____

- _____

6. Appreciate your supporters:

- _____

- _____

7. Help others succeed:

- _____

- _____

STEP 2: TAKING ACTION

Please write below the two most important things you will *do* for each of the *seven winning strategies*; include a completion date. To help you get started, here's an example for **leverage your strengths**:

☐ *I will complete the StrengthsFinder 2.0 assessment by March 31.*

1. Leverage your strengths:

☐ _____

☐ _____

2. Set stretch goals:

☐ _____

☐ _____

3. Work hard:

☐ _____

☐ _____

4. Stay balanced:

☐ _____

☐ _____

5. Be healthy:

☐ _____

☐ _____

6. Appreciate your supporters:

☐ _____

☐ _____

7. Help others succeed:

☐ _____

☐ _____

STEP 3: TRACKING RESULTS

Please keep track of what you accomplish by revisiting the *Taking action* section of *Your game plan* every three to six months. Feel free to change or update what you've written. After you complete each action, check the box, then add a new action if you wish.

STEP 4: TELLING YOUR STORY

If you're interested in telling your own success story to help inspire others, please let us know *what* you accomplished and *how* you did it; just e-mail a summary to:

Paul L. Corona

Author of *The Wisdom of Walk-Ons*

plcorona@wisdomofwalk-ons.com

Paul and his colleagues may share your story with others during speaking engagements, workshops, and coaching sessions. They may also publish it online and in paper form. Please note that by sharing your story, you're agreeing to these terms. Thanks in advance!

SPEAKING ENGAGEMENTS, WORKSHOPS, AND COACHING SESSIONS

If you're interested in experiencing *The Wisdom of Walk-Ons* live and in person, Paul Corona would be glad to speak with your large group, facilitate a workshop for your team, or provide coaching to individuals. Please contact him to discuss possibilities:

Paul L. Corona

Author of *The Wisdom of Walk-Ons*

plcorona@wisdomofwalk-ons.com

www.wisdomofwalk-ons.com

630-297-5120

REFERENCES

Adams, Gordon (2010). Personal interview.

Bleyer, Bob (2010). Personal interview.

Buckingham, Marcus (2007). *Go Put Your Strengths to Work: 6 Powerful Steps to Achieve Outstanding Performance*.

businteriors.com

cchs165.jacksn.k12.il.us

census.gov

cgu.edu

Covey, Stephen R. (2004). *The 8th Habit: From Effectiveness to Greatness*.

dictionary.com

Drucker, Peter (1999). "Managing Oneself," *Best of Harvard Business Review.*

Euripides. quotationspage.com/quote/2776.html, *The Quotations Page.*

Csikszentmihalyi, Mihaly (1990). *Flow: The Psychology of Optimal Experience*.

gallup.com

Goldsmith, Marshall (2009). *MOJO: How to Get It, How to Keep It, How to Get It Back If You Lose It.*

Hippocrates. quotationspage.com/quote/24184.html, *The Quotations Page.*

Insel, Paul M. and Roth, Walton T. (2011). *Connect Core Concepts in Health*, 12th edition.

Jackson, Phil (1995). *Sacred Hoops.*

jamesotoole.com

jcchs.org

marshallgoldsmithlibrary.com

Myer, Danny (2006). *Setting the Table: The Transforming Power of Hospitality in Business.*

O'Toole, James (2005). *Creating the Good Life: Applying Aristotle's Wisdom to Find Meaning and Happiness.*

Pizzitola, Alan (2010). Personal interview.

Rath, Tom (2007). *StrengthsFinder 2.0.*

Schwab, Charles (1997). "Succeeding with What You Have," *The Book of Business Wisdom: Classic Writings by the Legends of Commerce and Industry.*

stephencovey.com

strengthsfinder.com

tboc.com

nd.edu

nhhs.schoolloop.com/cms/page_view?d=x&piid=&v
pid=1211914114261

ua.edu

usc.edu

ushgnyc.com

usnews.com

Welch, Jack (1997). "Lessons for Success," *The Book of Business Wisdom: Classic Writings by the Legends of Commerce and Industry*.

Winfrey, Oprah. quotationspage.com/quote/31012.
html, *The Quotations Page.*

ACKNOWLEDGEMENTS

The Wisdom of Walk-Ons summarizes what I've learned, in 49 years of living, about how people truly succeed. This perspective can be traced to the countless family members, friends, teachers, classmates, coaches, teammates, mentors, and colleagues with whom I've been extremely fortunate to live and work. I wish I could thank all of you by name. Dad, Mom, Rick, Gary, Greg, and Cathy—thanks for giving me a solid foundation.

During the three years it has taken to conceptualize and write the book, I've become indebted to those who have listened to ideas, offered suggestions, given referrals, read drafts, and helped in other ways. I hope you all know how much I appreciate you and everything you've done.

The entire project has been a true team effort, so I'd like to recognize those whose contributions were particularly indispensable:

- My good friend Marty Kinna—who came up with the initial idea for *The Wisdom of Walk-Ons*. This never could have happened without you, brother.

- My wife and best friend Jen—who supported my passion, provided solid editing, demonstrated unwavering patience, and gave bone-crunching hugs with each bit of good news. I hope I enrich your life as much as you do mine.

- Our wonderful daughters Elizabeth and Margaret—who kept me focused with their contagious creativity and positive expectations. I know you'll enjoy a lifetime of success by doing your best and helping others do theirs.

- The three former walk-ons and stars of the show—Gordon Adams, Bob Bleyer, and Alan Pizzitola—who shared their fantastic stories and withstood my unending follow-up requests. You are role models to everyone who wants to do better.

- Coach Bobby Bowden and his attorney Rick Davis—who shared their expertise, offered guidance, and provided support. It's an honor to work with you.

- My colleague and friend Marianne Ryan—who devoured the literature and uncovered what some of the world's experts have said about the walk-ons' *seven winning strategies*. Thanks for your impeccable research, positive energy, and good humor.

- My colleagues and friends Steve Anzaldi and Kristi Hughes—who gave their great advice and talent from beginning to end. My hat is off to you.

- The CreateSpace publishing team—who brought the manuscript to life. Thanks for helping walk-on authors get in the game.

Paul L. Corona, MBA, EdD
Optimus Coaching
Chicago, Illinois

ABOUT THE AUTHOR

A UNIQUE PERSPECTIVE THAT INTEGRATES PRACTICE AND THEORY

Paul L. Corona—founder of Optimus Coaching and director of learning and organization development at Northwestern University—is an individual and organization development specialist with 27 years of management experience in *Fortune 300* corporations, a *Big 4* professional services firm, and major research universities. Before joining Northwestern, he was senior manager of professional development at Deloitte & Touche, manager of leadership and organization development at Lucent Technologies, and strategic marketing consultant in the Office of the Chancellor at Indiana University.

Paul holds a doctorate in higher education (with a specialty in custom programs of executive education) from Indiana University, an MBA in marketing from the University of Notre Dame, and a BA in advertising from Michigan State University. He has taught executives at the Kellogg School of Management; served as a guest lecturer in graduate courses at Northwestern University, Indiana University, and the University of Notre Dame; and taught undergraduates at Northwestern.

Paul is a member of the International Society for Performance Improvement, the American Society for Training & Development, and the Organization Development Network.

Made in the USA
Lexington, KY
14 February 2013